Collected Masonic Papers

2015 Transactions
of the
Louisiana Lodge of Research

Collected Masonic Papers

2015 Transactions of the
Louisiana Lodge of Research

MW. Clayton J. Borne, III, 33°, PGM
Worshipful Master
W. Michael R. Poll, PM
Secretary

Published by the Louisiana Lodge of Research
by agreement with
Cornerstone Book Publishers
Copyright as a collection © 2015 by Louisiana Lodge of Research
http://louisianalodgeofresearch.org

All rights reserved under International and Pan-American Copyright Conventions. No part of this book may be reproduced in any manner without permission in writing from the copyright holder, except by a reviewer, who may quote brief passages in a review.

Cornerstone Book Publishers
New Orleans, LA
www.cornerstonepublishers.com

ISBN:1613422695
ISBN-13:978-1-61342-269-4

MADE IN THE USA

Table of Contents

STRATEGIES FUNDAMENTAL TO THE SURVIVAL OF AMERICAN FREEMASONRY
by Robert G. Davis 1

THE IMPORTANCE OF THE EA DEGREE IN UNDERSTANDING OUR WORLD AS A MASTER MASON
by J. Quincy Gotte 16

THE MASONIC PHILOSOPHY: A LEGACY OF LIBERTY
by Clayton J. Borne, III 21

ALBERT PIKE 101
by Arturo de Hoyos 28

WHO ARE WE, AND WHERE DO WE STAND
by Robert L. Poll 33

IN THE PRESENCE OF FIRE
by River Folsom 37

THE ART OF CONVEYING A MESSAGE
by Jonathan K Poll 45

VIBRATIONS
by Elmo J. Barnes 49

WHY THE FC DEGREE
by J. Quincy Gotte 53

THE NEW ORLEANS ROOTS OF FREEMASONRY IN MOBILE, ALABAMA
by Wayne E. Sirmon 60

EARLY GRAND LODGE OF LOUISIANA PROCEEDINGS (PART ONE)
by Michael R. Poll 71

Past Masters of the Louisiana Lodge of Research

1989-90: William J. Mollere
1991: Ballard L. Smith
1992: Irving I. Berglass
1993: Philip J. Walker, Jr
1994: Beryl C. Franklin
1995: Ernest C. Belmont, Jr
1996: Thomas P. Brown
1997: Larry H. Moore
1998: Darrell L. Aldridge
1999: Edward W. Brabham, Jr
2000: Howard F. Entwistle, Jr
2001: Johnnie K. Hill
2002: Richard L. James
2003: Terrell Howes
2004: Glenn Cupit
2005: Robert Bazzell
2006: John Bellanger
2007: Jimmy Leger
2008: Ion Lazar
2009: Bill Richards
2010: Ricks Bowles
2011-15: Clayton J. Borne, III

The Grand Lodge of Louisiana, F&AM
P.O. Box 12357
5746 Masonic Drive
Alexandria, Louisiana. 71315-2357
Website: http://www.la-mason.com

M:W: William J. Mollere
Grand Master
R:W: Will P. Gray
Deputy Grand Master
R:W: Guy Jenkins
Grand Senior Warden
R:W: John T. Williamson
Grand Junior Warden
M:W: Woody D. Bilyeu, P.G.M.
Grand Treasurer
M:W: Roy B. Tuck, Jr., P.G.M.
Grand Secretary

Collected Masonic Papers

STRATEGIES FUNDAMENTAL TO THE SURVIVAL OF AMERICAN FREEMASONRY

by Robert G. Davis, 33°, G.C., PM
Secretary, Valley of Guthrie, OK
Past President, The Philalethes Society

This report is based on the following premises:

1) There are fundamental reasons why American Freemasonry is hovering on the edge of demise.
2) These reasons are identifiable, but represent challenges which, without reconciliation, may cause the fraternity to fall below a critical mass necessary to survival.
3) It is recognized some of these problems are systemic and will be difficult to reconcile.
4) It is recognized some of these problems are structural and cannot be reconciled without a change in Masonic law in most states.
5) Some of these problems are cultural and will not be overcome without new strategies and programs.
6) All of the problems must be addressed soon.

Several strategies critical to the fraternity's survival are available, and these should be well considered and implemented in a timely manner. If this can be done, certain other systemic and structural problems can also be resolved. However, if certain critical solutions are not put in place within the next few years, there is an impending risk the fraternity may not stay intact in its present adopted form in the United States.

Statement of Problems

The decline in American Freemasonry has been persistent for 56 years, and is not cyclical. Our declining numbers have not been reversed in spite of an aggressive number of programs and education efforts encompassing every aspect of the fraternity. These include regular ritual schools of instruction for degree teams, education in Masonry for both candidates and members, lodge officer leadership education, broad member participation programs, vast community participation efforts, focused family involvement programs, and local charitable programs which exceed $1 million annually in a number of states.

Yet, less than ten lodges in many states are growing; and less than 10% of the lodges in most Grand Jurisdictions have produced more than 4 candidates in any given year over the past 5 years through traditional raisings. It is estimated that up to 70% of the lodges in America can no longer confer the degrees, using their own lodge members, with adequate proficiency to impress candidates in a positive and meaningful way.

There are fundamental issues within the fraternity that have yet to be addressed. These issues are systemic, structural and cultural; and therefore can only be reconciled through selective strategies, followed by mass education.

Systemic Problems

Systemic problems are those which relate to the whole system, or body, of Masonry. These are common to every lodge and exist in every community. In Masonry, the most significant systemic problems are:

1) Masonry cannot provide the general public with a clear and simple definition of itself.
2) Masonry does not have a clearly understood public agenda.
3) Masonry does not have a clearly identifiable mission.
4) Men who are the most visible and active in the community do not appear to be Masons. Masons who are the most visible in the community do not appear to be the best known or most respected men in the community.
5) To the general public, the fraternity appears to be old and dying. Most people see it as an organization that used to be important.
6) It is still perceived by many that there is something secret, or even sinister, about Freemasonry.
7) There are many competing opportunities for a man's time; men perceive they have little free time.
8) Men no longer live in an exclusively male world.

Structural Problems

Structural problems are those which exist because of the nature of the organization itself; its habits, behaviors, paradigms, rules, and practices. The most significant structural problems in Masonry are:

1. It is complicated and time consuming to become a member.
2. Present approaches for attracting new members are non-aggressive and ineffectual.
3. Mandated memorization is outmoded and cumbersome.
4. Education and personal enlightenment emphasis are not central to most lodge teachings. Members do not know enough about Masonry to defend it from its most basic critics, nor discuss it in meaningful ways to their non-Masonic friends.
5. Membership is no longer exclusive. Almost anyone can join.
6. Men are often placed in officer positions with no leadership skills or experience. These men are the least capable of mandating change at Grand Lodge sessions, or reconciling outdated rules.
7. Ritual is too often mandated on officers rather than ritualists.
8. In many states, new members are excluded rather than encouraged to participate in lodge meetings.
9. Lodges offer meeting/activity agendas of little or no quality and thus provide no compelling reasons for members to participate.
10. There is no easy and practical method for eliminating old rules which are now damaging to the fraternity.
11. Meeting facilities are too often not appropriate to attract new members.
12. There are too few volunteers trying to keep too many Masonic organizations alive.
13. The fraternity promises a unique product that can be attractive to men, but fails to deliver on its promises.

Cultural Problems

Cultural problems are those which are inherent to the society in general, but have a large effect on an organization's potential for success. Some of the significant cultural problems facing Masonry are:

1) Sons no longer follow their fathers into Masonry. Men are often not aware there is Masonic legacy in their family.
2) Men who work in white collar occupations perceive Masonry as an irrelevant organization.
3) Masonry offers too many rules and too little flexibility for today's fast paced world.
4) Masonry is too often racially exclusive, and therefore too risky for upwardly mobile males to join.
5) Masonry is considered too secretive and eccentric, and not open to public scrutiny.
6) Masonry is perceived to offer no economic benefits or connections.
7) Masonry is considered exclusively male and therefore at risk of wives acceptance.
8) Men no longer join organizations which offer no tangible benefits, or any compelling reasons to belong.

All of the above problems represent staggering challenges to the fraternity. Yet, as challenging as they may be, each can at least be addressed and incorporated into the blueprint for our institution. But time is of the essence.

Solutions fundamental to the survival of Freemasonry must be implemented by Masonic leaders soon. There is precious little time left for education or debate on how best to solve many of these strategic issues. Because time is so critical a factor (the age and impending mortality of our active members threatens to close too many lodges before any renaissance can occur), the leadership of Grand Lodge may even need to consider mandating changes essential to survival and then educate the craft after these solutions are mandated.

Once again, there is a fundamental position in this crucial matter:

There are identifiable reasons why the Masonic fraternity in the United States is on the edge of demise. For the fraternity to survive, the essential problems which are contributing to its demise must be resolved as quickly and efficiently as possible.

Strategic and Structural Measures Essential to the Short Term Survival and Stability of American Freemasonry

Since time is of the essence, a movement will need to be created within the fraternity which will uniformly address organizational paradigms currently eroding the integrity of Freemasonry as an institution. Any recommendations advanced that will prove effective in shifting paradigms or changing certain behavioral practices will, by necessity, also need to focus on the organizational structure of the fraternity itself.

Therefore, Grand Lodges and Symbolic Lodges will both need to buy into these changes. Grand Masters, representing Grand Lodges through the authority given them by the Laws, Constitutions, Charges and Landmarks of Masonry (along with the follower-ship and influence of elected Grand Lodge Trustees) will need to sanction certain practices so that local lodges will feel they have been given permission to implement these at home. Symbolic lodges, represented by the sitting Worshipful Masters (and their active Past Masters) will need to concur that certain organizational changes are both necessary and in the best interest of the fraternity at home.

Actions to be taken must be focused on four principle areas of Masonic concern:

I. Lodge Empowerment Tools
II. Influencing Needed Changes in Masonic Law
III. Ritual Adaptation and Diversity
IV. Targeted Groups/Special Classes
V. Restoration of Traditional Practices

Specific recommended actions are listed here within each of these broad themes, as follows:

I. LODGE EMPOWERMENT TOOLS

A significant and dramatic change in lodge practices is essential to regain a quality fraternal experience and establish an attractive and compelling environment in which to attract new members. There are several very significant actions lodges can take without requirement of legislation, or change, in the state laws governing the fraternity. However, because there is an ubiquitous perception that Grand Lodges control the practices of their constituent lodges, it is necessary that official action be taken that will empower lodges to make adaptations according to their own constituted authority.

Granting Self Governance—It is recommended that Grand Masters issue decisions and adopt practices that will enable constituent lodges to make certain changes, or adaptations, governing how they attract prospective members, how they define their own lodge joining process, and how they practice their ritual. While voluntary in its adoption, such official decree will enable lodges, through their own self governance, to decide for themselves on several important matters of Masonic practice with their respective Grand Jurisdictions. Regrettably, most Masonic Codes focus on lodge prohibitions; yet there are many permitted practices in Freemasonry. Lodge Masters are often reluctant to try things that the Code is silent on, assuming it might be prohibited. What is needed for lodges is a permitted practices book in every jurisdiction.

Specifically, it is recommended that Grand Masters and/or Grand Lodges:

1. Authorize a program of "Selective Invitation" whereby lodge members may recommend individuals for membership and officially invite these prospects to join. This will enable lodges to target those individuals within the community who are most likely to have an interest in fraternity, or the most able to help the lodge be successful in the future.
2. Provide for a broader interpretation of the meaning of demonstrated proficiency in the memorization lectures required of candidates. Rote memorization is one of the American innovations in Masonry. Traditional methods of demonstrating proficiency such as presenting papers, describing one's understanding of a degree, being mentored and schooled by knowledgeable peers, etc., have been determined the world over to provide a better means of education, understanding, and light in Masonry than rote memorization.

3. Eliminate mandated time requirements between degrees so that candidates are given the sole responsibility in determining how fast they progress through Masonry.
4. In Grand Jurisdictions that prohibit alcoholic beverages in lodge buildings, relax rules governing alcoholic beverages to provide that Masons can be together at social functions, festive boards, banquets, etc. in lodge social settings not unlike that which is typically available to other civic, organizational, and professional affinity groups. The festive board is the oldest practice in Masonry. It is detrimental to the fraternity that social drinking among brothers is prohibited in Masonic buildings.
5. Encourage lodges to consider their most able members for officer-ship and formally acknowledge that such qualified leaders may serve more than one term as officers and Worshipful Masters. Our Masonic historical traditions clearly show that men typically served multiple years in mastership of their lodge.
6. In Grand Lodges where only one candidate can receive the degrees, authorize multiple candidates to receive the degrees of Masonry at one time; thus encouraging men to bring their friends into the fraternity with them; and promoting that mystic tie that binds among those who receive their degrees together.
7. Encourage flexibility and creativity in the use of music, lighting, and effects used during lodge degrees to enhance the impact and influence the degree can have as a transforming experience in the candidate's life.
8. Encourage the use of music as a regular part of the practice of lodge meetings. Masonic Odes sung in lodge are among the oldest practices in Freemasonry.

II.   INFLUENCING NEEDED CHANGES IN MASONIC LAW

It is recommended that Grand Masters and Grand Lodges create certain resolutions for change essential to the survival of their constituent lodges. Such changes will require the implementation of a broad education program and focused communication with voting delegates to ensure favorable legislation is adopted to bring about these needed changes.

Specifically, the following kinds of legislative changes are recommended for adoption in Grand Jurisdictions that presently have prohibitions:

1. Remove language in Masonic laws which require Worshipful Masters and Wardens to be able to confer degrees as a duty of their respective offices. Lodge officers should be selected on the basis of leadership skills and experience; not on their ability to memorize ritual words.
2. Revise codes so that Entered Apprentices and Fellow crafts may participate in the business of lodge. It is not necessary these men be given voting privileges, but it is essential that they have the right to sit in lodge every time it is opened for stated business.
3. Revise Masonic laws to permit all monitorial lectures to be presented in their entirety in audio, visual, and electronic formats.
4. Revise codes to provide for the adoption and use of cipher keys as an aid in ritual proficiency.
5. Revise Masonic laws where necessary to provide that all amendments to Masonic law shall be in full force and effect when adopted by a simple majority of the members present at an Annual Communication of Grand Lodge. Eliminate super majority voting options.
6. Eliminate laws providing for proxy voting by delegates of Grand Lodge.

III. RITUAL ADAPTATION AND DIVERSITY

The ritual is the mold that holds the structure of Freemasonry together and makes it uniquely different from other community organizations. It is the foundation upon which one actually realizes personal and spiritual growth as a Freemason. The problem is that fewer and fewer lodges have the ability to confer all three Degrees in their entirety. The honored men whom almost every lodge once had to teach the ritual are now too few in number to serve effectively the fraternity. Once a lodge loses its ability to confer degrees, it also loses its inspiration to encourage men to join. As the ritual is lost, so is the lodge.

1. It is recommended the lectures of the degrees be digitized for use in lodge, and every lodge be mandated to own the

equipment for showing the same to its candidates. It is recommended the historical (lantern slide) images be complimented with contemporary images so that the visual icons continue the tradition as well as provide an identifiable association with contemporary times.
2. As lectures are no longer performed in many lodges, much of the symbolism and meaning of Masonry is no longer delivered to candidates. To address this problem, the monitorial lectures of the Craft Degrees should be performed regionally on a quarterly schedule by a team of excellent ritualists selected by the Grand Lodge. It is important that places be selected across the Grand Jurisdiction so that no brother is more than 50 miles from a quarterly lecture site.
3. Grand Lodges should encourage alternatives to rote memorization as a test of candidate proficiency. Papers prepared and presented in lodge and/or extemporary explanations of what the candidate understands about each degree are equally significant. It is estimated that 80% of those who do not advance beyond the 1st Degree do not advance because of rote memory requirements.
4. Grand Lodges should authorize selected lodges within each Grand Jurisdiction to confer the degrees using a different ritual than that formally adopted by the Grand Lodge. Permitting several ritual alternatives such as English, Scottish, and Irish workings would add much ritual interest to American Masonry.
5. In cities that are characterized by a diverse culture, Grand Lodges should authorize specialty lodges to confer the work in foreign languages. This would attract more men within the same ethnic cultures to join the fraternity.

IV. TARGETED GROUPS/SPECIALTY CLASSES

There are two stubborn paradigms in American Freemasonry that have not served the fraternity well since the middle of the 20th century. One has been the insistence that every lodge is made for every man; the other, that more members are better than a few members in each lodge. The result of the first paradigm is that men are too often encouraged to become Masons who have little more than a curiosity about it, and have not qualified themselves to be duly and truly prepared to be Masons. Further, men who otherwise have little or nothing in common in a community are forced into association together where Masonry is often their only shared interest.

Secondly, during the first half of the 20th century many individual lodges grew to memberships of hundreds and even thousands of men. While this seemingly economic boon resulted in the building of magnificent Masonic structures, these same lodges had no practical means of providing fraternal care and attention to all members; or maintaining fraternal relationships on a scale necessary to distinguish the fraternity from a church or civic organization. In lodges comprised of hundreds of members, those members who actively participate have never known more than a handful of their own brothers. With the ever increasing rate of mobility in jobs among all employment classifications over the past 50 years, many members in American lodges have had regular contact with less than 20% of their own lodge's total membership for their entire lives.

Until we have a meaningful fraternal relationship with all our brothers, we can hardly call our organization fraternal. Yet, being fraternal is precisely what distinguishes us from the rest of the community.

1. It is recommended that Grand Masters and Grand Lodges aggressively encourage the formation of new lodges. This will provide a venue for those brothers who want a different kind of Masonic experience but consistently run into rigidity and intolerance in their lodges to form new lodges around their own fraternal expectations. New lodges, with the energy and vision which generally accompanies them, also replace defunct lodges and help offset those existing lodges that are ineffective and exist in name only.
2. It is recommended that Grand Lodges encourage the formation of traditional lodges, a concept that was established more than a decade ago to bring a menu of best Masonic practices worldwide to the American experience. More information can be attained at www.masonicrestoration.com
3. It is recommended that Grand Lodges encourage the formation of affinity lodges; i.e., lodges made up of men in the same occupations, in the same professions, in the same hobbies, etc.

Such lodges have always existed in British, European, and South American Masonry. This allows like-minded men to enjoy the traditional, organizational, and ceremonial aspects of Freemasonry, while placing a high emphasis on the fraternalism and social value of their overall common interests.

4. It is recommended that Lodges and Grand Lodges who are engaged in forming new lodges encourage the ideal lodge size in the future to be less than 100 members; and if that number is reached, the lodge be encouraged to hold at that level or split its member base to from a second lodge. In metropolitan areas, it is far better to have 100 lodges with 50 members than 10 lodges with 500 members. Small groups of men tend to maintain meaningful interaction and fraternalism within their group, and thus regularly participate in it. Large groups of men tend to value the overall purpose and values of the organization, but are generally passive to individual participation in it.

V. RESTORATION OF TRADITIONAL PRACTICES

American Freemasonry currently stands at a crossroads while facing its most difficult historical challenge. If it can overcome this challenge, it can re-create itself with a firm sense of purpose and identity; and speak with a powerful voice in America's future. The alternative is that it will degenerate into a de-ritualized social club or service organization, and become like every other community organization.

The challenge we face is that a majority of today's Masons view Freemasonry and its purpose in the same way that they experienced it over the past 70 years—as a large fraternal organization, involving family, and meeting primarily social and charitable needs. There is nothing wrong with such an organization, but that definition is far too broad to be called a fraternity. It fails to address the core purpose of its existence—to provide intellectual and moral education and unite men in noble pursuit of the highest social, spiritual, and philosophical ideals. Without knowing it, we moved our fraternity off its center in the 20th century.

This happened in the relatively short span of time between the WW II era men and today's Millennials. Our Masonic culture evolved into two prevailing attitudinal groups, largely at odds with each other. These two groups can be characterized as the "old hard liners" or the "old mentality," and the "new radicals," or "new mentality." And since most Masons are inactive in the sense they are content to hold membership cards and pay dues, the small minority who are active tend to govern lodges and Grand Lodges. These men are highly politicized about the fraternity, and generally ignorant of its history and purpose. Both groups are highly threatening to the interests and future of American Freemasonry. If unity is not resolved soon, Masonry's future is very bleak.

The "hard liners" have gained the upper hand in most lodges where Masonry is dying. These men are largely composed of Past Masters at the local level who are opposed to any change in the programs of their lodge. They represent the less than 10 active members who regularly attend lodge, and seem set at driving their lodge into the ground rather than adopting any new programs, or evaluating current ones. Their fatalistic approach requires no effort and dismisses all initiatives coming from Grand Lodge as radical heresy. They are fatal to their lodge.

The radicals are those who bought into flawed and misguided sentiments claiming that the moral instruction offered through Masonic ritual had become totally useless in modern society. In areas where the radicals have prevailed, usually more commonly in Grand Lodge leadership circles, innovations like one day classes, solicitation, reduction in membership qualifications, multiple black balls, etc., have damaged the uniqueness of Freemasonry, and lowered the quality of men to the point many lodges no longer have the power to enact the most worthy of social changes. The understanding of what constitutes the timeless nature of Freemasonry that has given it strength and durability through the centuries has been almost wholly obscured by the prevailing model of North American Masonry.

It is important to understand that these attitudes and issues, while systemic, are political. They can be reconciled through knowledge, education, and awareness. Fortunately, there is a third culture arriving on the American Masonic scene that can overcome both of the above mentioned forces.

There is a new growing third political trend in American Masonry, representing a group of younger, more professional men that can be referred to as "moderate reformists." This group is general disappointed with the state of Freemasonry and sees the dangers and follies of both reactionary fatalism and radical ignorance. These new guys seek to improve Masonry by legitimate means, with a focus on what is most important about Freemasonry and what it can offer to men and society. These men currently comprise the intellectual core of Freemasonry, and are well informed and connected through the internet.

This third group can be differentiated from the reactionaries because it:

a) Holds no illusions about a status quo that must be maintained or a golden past that must be returned to at all costs,
b) Seeks no radical changes, but rather seeks to preserve all that is related to the roots of Freemasonry,
c) Seeks to change only the deviations that have developed in American Masonry over the last century which have led to its demise.
d) Seeks to bring the best global practices of Masonry to the American experience.

To serve the interests and vision of moderate reformers, thereby neutralizing the fatalistic trends that crept into the American Masonic culture during the 20th century, the following strategies will need to be employed:

1. Grand Lodges should look to local lodges for solutions and sanction local efforts to adapt programs that fit local member desires and needs.
2. Lodges should be encouraged to become constituent partners with Grand Lodge rather than subservient entities.
3. Masonic Codes should be codified to eliminate all unnecessary and trivial rules that restrict the sovereignty of the individual Lodge to enable each lodge to be as successful as it can within its group and within the ancient customs and landmarks of Freemasonry.
4. Grand Lodges and local Lodges should develop a more attractive and sophisticated public image for the fraternity that appeals to qualified men and young professionals. Public image programs should focus on shaping the kind of men that will make up the next generation of Masons.

5. Much emphasis must be placed on candidate education programs designed to attract qualified leaders into leadership positions so that future leaders can advance our foundational causes.
6. Model member education programs addressing the systemic lack of a meaningful system of candidate and member education should be developed nationally and widely distributed among lodges. Such a system will shape the way the fraternity defines itself and its role.
7. Fraternal leaders should make a comprehensive study of Continental European and Scandinavian Masonic practices to determine why/how these countries have been highly successful at developing and sustaining membership, as well as providing a sophisticated image to the public.
8. All Grand Lodges and Masonic leaders should encourage the development of a "best practices" attitude within the fraternity and give lodges the freedom to implement programs that have already proven to be successful in other jurisdictions and countries.

The bottom line is that it is of utmost importance to restore Masonry to its original purpose and timeless nature—that of teaching good men to subdue their passions, become Masters over themselves, and reborn as better men.

The Vision

American Freemasonry should be an institution which appeals to men of quality and good rapport, without regard for race, religion or creed; men who profess a faith in a supreme being and are well recommended.

Our lodges should be places where brothers are anxious to regularly attend because doing so is an event which educates them, inspires them, enlightens them and delights them. Freemasonry should be a place of great connections; a place where we meet our friends, our peers and mentors; where, together, we work out the great problems of life and our own self-transformation.

A Masonic Lodge should be a place of education and enlightenment, consistently delivering, by ritual, symbols, allegory, study and practical magic, a moral discipline founded on the highest standards of ethics, honesty, and strength of character.

A lodge should be a place where younger men and older men meet on a foundation of mutual respect, forged from both the familiar and the unfamiliar; where both learn and connect with each other, respecting that neither's path is entirely right or wrong.

A Lodge should be a place of harmony and fraternity, where respect for one another and for the ideals of fraternity are the highest aims; practicing the tenets of brotherly love in a sanctuary of good will and association.

A Lodge should be a place of joy, entertainment, and refreshment; where learning and work is balanced with fellowship and feasting; delivering delight and fraternal conviviality in a haven of mutual respect and toleration.

THE IMPORTANCE OF THE EA DEGREE IN UNDERSTANDING OUR WORLD AS A MASTER MASON

by J. Quincy Gotte 32°
Worshipful Master, Rudolph Krause Lodge #433
Treasurer, Valley of Lake Charles, LA

I recall how I felt after being raised a Master Mason. I was excited to learn all there was to know about Freemasonry, and couldn't wait to receive my first lesson as a Master Mason. But I must confess that even as the MM Degree, with all its drama and symbolic allegories, is presented as the apex of the Freemason's journey, the EA Degree still fascinates me. Ever since I was raised a Master Mason, I've always walked with the EA Degree close beside me. There were times that I wondered if I was really a Master Mason. I mean, we all know what makes us a Master Mason, and I guess I'm as much a Master Mason as the next by those terms. But to be truthful and honest, because I don't always feel as though I've mastered myself or even fully understand how to, a part of me still feels like I am an Entered Apprentice Mason. I used to be troubled by these feelings, and couldn't put my finger on why a part of me felt compelled to be ashamed of feeling like an Entered Apprentice, and a part of me was completely ok with it and excited to be one, or at least feel like one. So I decided to devote some thought in understanding more clearly as to how a Master Mason can still feel like an Entered Apprentice Mason, and why one would feel compelled to under value the position of an Entered Apprentice Mason.

As I pondered and studied, and became more pensive; I realized that this is not off base at all with "The Great Aim" of Freemasonry, which will be alluded to going forward. As a matter of thought, I believe it is safe to say that most Master Masons feel as though they are still an Entered Apprentice Mason at times— and rightfully so; after all, the Entered Apprentice Degree is all about coming to a realization about our rudimentary connection to this wondrous imperfect world by which we are bound to throughout our entire lives, and how we must work with our disassembling elements and build a perfect Temple.

THE CITY AND THE TOWER

The realization of our base nature and its continuance is indispensable to our work as Master Masons. So as a Mason, there is value in our base nature and its connection to this imperfect world. Striving to rise above this world and become or return to something much greater is naturally instilled within our being. This raw ambition, which is so much a part of mankind, is what employs our actions and enables us to achieve extraordinary feats. We can read in the book of Genesis a story about the building of the Tower of Babel. It tells us how the people of that city worked together in one accord to build a tower so that they could elevate their physical status to align with how they viewed themselves to be. Now there are many lessons to be learned in this story which range anywhere from communication of mankind to a contrast of the New Jerusalem spoken of in St. John's Apocalypse. But ultimately, this story teaches that success was not realized by the manner in which their ambition was employed. I prefer to view the story of Nimrod's city as displaying man's efforts to rise above himself, climbing and striving to obtain the Holiness that is beyond his grasp; using a tower or temple built by his own physical hand driven by his ill-applied ambition. Nimrod's city is a perfect picture of man's base nature at work and its failure through vanity.

In contrast, we can find a story of a very different city in St. John's Apocalypse found in the last book of the Christian Bible. It speaks of a Holy city, not built by the physical hand of man driven by his ambition, but prepared by the Holiness and sacrifice made by the Christ; coming down to meet mankind so that the Holiness of God, blessed be He, can dwell within and amongst mankind without the need of a temple or tower to go to or climb, because It and all It encompasses will be the Temple.

Now if we are not careful, we may wrongfully assume that the work of our hands, along with our ambition, is an unfulfilling work of vanity; but this is not what should be concluded by the aforementioned stories. Both cities have their purpose and place, and one cannot exist without the connection and continuance of certain elements of the other. What needs to be noticed is the ill-placed ambition of man in his base self, and how the correction of his employment of that ambition needs to be realized. Our base nature and our physical elements are not the ungodliness that causes us to fail, but should be viewed as the potential foundation provided in order to prepare a realization and connection to the next level of the Temple, and should not be viewed as a stepping stone to be left behind.

A CONCEPT OF AWAKENING

If humanity's happiness was provided within the rudimentary connection to this material realm alone, then conforming to the demands of this corporeal world would be the key to fulfillment, which life itself disproves; therefore, we are not completely of this corporeal realm, but are 1/3 of it at the very most. Also, to be completely consumed by a desire to leave or rise above this world by grasping at spiritual enigmas to the point that we disconnect and isolate ourselves from all who are not seeking those same enigmas, will cause the pendulum to swing the opposite way concluding the same results to be the realization of a lack of fulfillment, because we are at the very most 1/3 spiritual. So, an understanding of where the divisional lines are and how to connect them is essential to our Masonic fulfillment. If you recall within the *Louisiana Masonic Monitor*, this is alluded to by the WM in his communication to every candidate in the preparation room, but usually not initially understood. So it is clear that before growth and fulfillment can take place, one must realize the divisional lines within one's self.

THE STEP

The Entered Apprentice Degree is the first step within this realization, and pertains to the laws of nature, society, and Brotherhood. It is the first step away from barbarism, and into Light. It is an instructed step in the dark, and a provisional portion of Light revealing that you are not alone in your obligation and work. This is what makes the EA Degree so important and continuously relevant within the work of a Mason. This Degree pertains to a symbolic dislodging of one's original connection to the social and physical ties to the mass populace, and how one is to work within it going forward. In the Degree, a "silentude" should be experienced within the candidate's present darkness, and his unknown desire for Light is spoken of and requested for him to ensure the silence of his base desire. The Degree signifies a type of conception or birth, which begins when the candidate realizes he is separated and in darkness. The first divisional line is realized, and a separation of the elements is performed in order to alchemically change the first element, and prepare it for a future connection to the next Degree. Just as our great symbol is never permanently separated from itself or fused forever to itself, but is transformed through a gradual separation and reconnection; such is this process alluded to of our self throughout each Degree.

So, we must conclude that passing from one Degree to another does not mean that we have moved beyond the previous Degree, but have gone through it and continue to carry its work and Light with us. It is clear that the Entered Apprentice Degree is the foundation degree of Freemasonry, and should be rightfully valued as such.

A CONCEPT OF DIVISION

One commonality with all the ancient mysteries is the basic division of man. In Manly P Hall's lecture on San Juan's (also known as St. John of the Cross) *"The Dark Night of the Soul"* it states that *"man has three natures, or parts, of which the highest and first is essentially spiritual; the second, psychic, or belonging to the sphere of soul; and the third, material, bodily or corporeal, relating to the realm of body."* It is also stated in that same text saying, *"Materialism is not man's natural way; it is a way forced upon him by exterior factors, or by the confusion in his own nature and life."* Other examples of the division can be found in books like Rabbi Joseph Gikatilla's *"Gates of Light"*, where it explains the elements of man are divided and identified as *"the Nefesh (the living force), the Ruach (the spirit), and the Neshamah (the Divine soul)."* The division of the corporeal is also evident in relation to the sun working through the Zodiac. It is noted in 32° Robert Hewitt Brown's *"Stellar Theology and Masonic Astronomy"*, that *"the Royal Arch is supported by the three Cardinal Points of the Zodiac, which consists of the Vernal and Autumnal equinoctial points at the base, and the solstice point at the summit, of which the three are emblematic of the three Pillars of the Lodge."*

These divisions are important to life as we learn and know it. There is an understanding of time and course, and any imbalances of the seasons can be devastating. Now when we allow the corporeal elements to employ our psychic and spiritual energy to render profit to the corporeal only, we are dividing ourselves in a way that is cultivating confusion; one third then usurps the other two thirds, and we then suffer a deficit within our whole self. This lesson is alluded to in the explanation of the three Great Lights and the three lesser lights; as well as the 24 inch Gauge. So, the only way to create order through the chaos of confusion is to properly identify our 3 dimensional make up. We must learn how to properly pull apart and reconnect the three by understanding how one serves the other, and also by understanding the importance of the role of each and the course by which they must work. The goal of the Entered Apprentice is to begin and prepare himself for the search of Truth.

We are not required to completely understand what is in the plans or the mind of the G.A.O.T.U. That would be like trying to understand a 9 dimensional concept with a 3 dimensional mind; besides, we are able to exercise faith by these restrictions. What is required of us is to understand our 3 dimensional existences, and to understand the relevance of each one before we can properly connect it to the other. Once this is accomplished and mastered, another dimension can be introduced to us; until then, what good would it be to have access to 9 or 10 dimensions if the 3 or 4 we now have access to confuse us?

"...until quietism is attained, through certain continuing discipline, no individual is in a position to know the truth. For the truth is not something that is instantly available in spite of what we are; it is something ultimately available because of what we are. The mere fact that we seek truth, that we believe in it and long for it, or that we create definitions for it—this compound process is not sufficient. The individual, to attain to the state of true internal enlightenment, must recover first from confusion." "Search for reality: Part 1- The Dark Night of the Soul- Lectures on Personal Growth"- Manly P. Hall

So in order to understand our world as a Master Mason, we must remember the lessons taught as an Entered Apprentice. Growth can change the dynamics of how everything in our life operates. So the things that we've mastered in the past, now take on a new characteristic in our growth. And because we do grow, there will always be a need of discipline to accompany that growth. This reminds us that we should always be willing to dislodge ourselves from the mass populace and return to a lonely silent place, and keep the lessons of this Degree within our work and knowledge; sizing ourselves up against its moral code ensuring us that our foundation is still within its circumscribed boundaries.

"Light partakes of both life and action; it is the sphere of blending" "Melchizedic and the Mystery of Fire"- Manly P. Hall

THE MASONIC PHILOSOPHY: A LEGACY OF LIBERTY
(Delivered at the World Conference of Grand Lodges, 11/20/2015)
by Clayton J. Borne, III, 33°, PGM (LA)
Worshipful Master, Louisiana Lodge of Research

Liberty has been defined as the power of the will to follow the dictates of its unrestricted choice, the freedom from all restraints, except such as is justly imposed by law. It is this unrestricted choice that you and I, as Freemasons, are taught to foster or develop. We encourage awareness through our rational conscious, in order to change our daily conduct in our journey to Enlightenment and understanding the meaning of Life.

We live in an ever changing world; a world in which forces appear to threaten our most fundamental concepts of freedom. There appears to be however a renewed interest and universal appeal for the steadfast consistency of the principles found in the teachings of our Order. Our Brotherhood's stability over the ages has been and will continue to be our core belief in the existence of a Supreme Being or Monotheism, accompanied by The Doctrine of Transubstantiation or a belief in a spirit life after death and our ability as mortal beings to have our spirit reunited with our Creator, who we as Freemasons describe as "The Grand Architect Of The Universe" and live reunited in a life without end. This conviction allows for a personal transformation by each of us, to change from a self centered existence, to an unselfish caring philosophy by which we live our lives. This Cornerstone conviction of our Order, by definition, gives our spiritual brotherhood of Freemasonry a logical imperative or a rational reason to exist. "Unity with God" by virtue of our faith is the liberating object of our Masonic discipline.

I.   CORE VALUES

This core principle mandates a philosophy of mutual respect for our fellow man, namely the freedom to treat others as you wish to be treated. It is the predicate necessary for the development of a disciplined yet free society. Also this philosophy is at the center of understanding the Masonic discipline and the Masonic way of life, specifically to keep our passions in due bounds with all mankind especially our brother Masons. There are Societies today unwilling to accept intellectual freedom and will not tolerate those who are in opposition to their beliefs. Our tiled Lodges throughout history have been and continue to be a safe venue for the expressions of intellectual freedom.

However before we discuss the implementation of the intellectual freedom and its legacy to each of our lives, we must ask ourselves the question, "Are all men capable of understanding the cornerstone principle of our Masonic Order?" I submit to each of you my brothers that although maturing societies offer an opportunity, the Masonic philosophy can only flourish if the primitive or basic fundamental needs of our fellow man are satisfied. These fundamental considerations are described in terms of a hierarchy of needs, the analysis of which reveals a complex roadmap to understanding human existence. This is exactly why we as Masons must accept that man must satisfy these primal needs before he will concern himself with the basic procuring of freedom.

In an analysis of diverse societies, we find in man a basic commonality in his attempt to individually satisfy his fundamental needs. The satisfaction of these considerations is necessary in allowing him to develop physically and physiologically. In a primitive state, man struggles to satisfy these needs such as food and water. He innately senses the need for safety and security, not only for himself but for those of his immediate family. He craves social acceptance and the securing of social needs such as love, appreciation and companionship. With these basic needs satisfied, the individual is then able to move forward and develop "self esteem" or the valuing and defining the concept of "Self". Without the ability to value and respect himself, man is unable to respect and value the rights of others.

Absent satisfaction of these core needs, rationalization and freedom of thought is severely diminished. In other words, how do we as a brotherhood expect to instill values on an individual and subsequently the society in which he lives, when that society is plagued with hunger and oppression? It is virtually impossible to achieve social progress and bring a man to an enlightened state with these impediments confronting him in his daily life.

II. EDUCATIONAL FREEDOM

Further, it has been written that no one is truly free that has not been educated. The South African philosopher/political leader, Nelson Mandela said "Education is the most powerful weapon which you can use to change the world". Without education human existence is destined to remain in the shackles of slavery. Through education we are able to actively satisfy our fundamental needs. We are also through education able to hold fast to the basic concepts of Liberty and learn to resist the innate desire to judge with bias those whose beliefs are different from our own. We also learn to objectively assimilate into our lives those principles of the good which are developed for our own moral betterment. Our brotherhood's growth in society especially in the emerging countries of the world is based on the advocating of education, for all of society which will then mature into a culture or society that learns to treat others, as we wish to be treated. The Philosopher, "Immanuel Kant", (1724 to 1804), in one of his last writings questions "What is Enlightenment?" His response is one word, "Freedom". Education is truly the liberating road to freedom.

III. FUNDAMENTAL LIBERTIES

History has shown that despite the attempts to educate and teach mutual respect, historically the development of most society emanates or grows out of the chaos and conflict of man's struggles with one another. The ancient philosopher Aristotle discusses this social development as "Theories of the Good" wherein Aristotelian thinking states that a good life is a virtuous life and virtue consist in being willing to subordinate one's private end to the common welfare. Societies that developed with this philosophy created a disciplined social order wherein happiness is found in an alliance of virtue and common ideals.

Albert Pike addresses this concept of Liberty and describes it as the Award or Prize of a hard fought battle. Aristotle, as a contrast states that a truly virtuous man does not struggle to be virtuous. Pike submits an opposing philosophy, that there exists a great inequity in the well being of men with most struggling for, as we have previously discussed, a mere existence. He takes the position that without the noble struggle, it is impossible for people to acquire virtue and without a struggle it is impossible to truly appreciate the concept of liberty. Freedom that is given to us at no cost or without a price is taken for granted.

It is our Brotherhood's duty to protect and preserve this philosophy which in turn will promote an appreciation of freedom, more particularly a free disciplined society restricted only by just laws.

IV. THE IDEOLOGY OF FREEMASONRY AND CULTURAL DIVERSITY

Daily we are faced with the confrontation of choices between good and evil. These choices are affected and shaped by the added consideration of cultural relevance. To understand our brothers' motivations, his choices and his behavior we must try to understand his individual culture and beliefs. The United States a country primarily of immigrants and their descendants is a collection of diverse cultures. Disharmony comes when these various cultures or ways of living come into contact with one another. It takes the acceptance of basic moral values for diverse peoples to live in harmony. Freemasonry is ideologically that which opposes immoral ideas that suppress the positive development of humanity and spiritual enlightenment.

The transformation of society is in reality a transformative process wherein we as a brotherhood are encouraged to advocate a change in ourselves from one state of conscious to another. In due course we develop an automatic subconscious conviction to a state of thought that creates a tolerance and acceptance of various diversities. Simply put the pursuit of this virtue will create a change in our perception of life.

Also, without the struggle for freedom by virtuous men, society will become complacent in the appreciation of his liberties. Our Masonic ritual teaches each of us not to fall victim to this human tendency. Error and disappointment are the designs of providence that leads to truth and happiness. Each one of us has a responsibility to ourselves, as well as society, to strive for moral values by which we can all live in harmony.

V. THREATS TO FREE SOCIETIES

In these Societies that have prospered as a result of unique issues of conflict such as the United States and its' American Revolution, the reality of free institutions, stable constitutional government, comfortable living and freedom have helped to insure that the virtuous concepts of Liberty, procured in that struggle will not being taken for granted.

As we strive to cultivate integrity in our personal lives and collectively in society, our efforts however meet with constant resistance. As appalling as it may be, society today mirrors a reflection of disrespect, and unappreciative and uncaring cancer that migrates into all aspects of our respective culture. The cure as with all other social problems is education, the lack of which have prevented generations from appreciating the opportunity for and the privileges of living in a free society.

The Masonic ideals and their influence on society through the ages have been exerted in no better or nobler purpose or cause than the ageless struggle by the Brotherhood for "Liberty, Equality and Fraternity". President George Washington, Benjamin Franklin, and the Marquis de Lafayette and many other leaders such as Bolivar, Garibaldi and Juarez embraced freemasonry and its philosophy, finding honor in their association and commitment to it. They literally guaranteed the success of these ideals with their lives. Our Fraternity has been the champions of the oppressed people with the object being the emancipation of mankind from every form of tyranny. Within our lodges Freedom, especially in thought and expressions, was freely encouraged. That freedom made it possible for the natural progression by our Brotherhood toward a transformed life as is exemplified by the Rituals of our Order.

It must be emphasized however that the humanist philosophy so prevalent in society poses obstructions to our Masonic ideals. The basic concept of Liberty has always had an aggressive enemy which knocks at the inner door of our lodges. It is the self centered, selfish concepts evidenced by Pride, Falsehood and Ambition which are the fundamental individual components fostering the concept of entitlements. This philosophy is in direct opposition to the principles of our Order.

The entitlement belief is the direct result of the modernist negative empowerment doctrine that there is no rational basis for values. Despite our Masonic brotherhood's continued efforts to promote integrity, the value system of society has been eroded. Much of society values become problematic, in other words nothing is truly good or bad. It's all a matter of opinion. We must of necessity ask then how and why have principles? Do as you please or whatever you can rationalize as being right. It is only when people do the right thing freely can we have confidence in their character. If they act out of principles such as truth, benevolence and productiveness as taught in our Fraternity; then we know their actions resulted from good character and the principles of liberty are preserved.

The world in which we now live is dramatically changing. Idealistic principles are important to fewer and fewer people. We demand of our leaders, honesty, but we don't really expect them to be honest. Societies have become weakened where honesty becomes relative and rationalization of all conduct is the norm. We are often saying that our communities are civilized societies of law, but too often laws are broken and then attempts are made to justify the actions. That logic is corruptive, destructive but most importantly contagious.

Prevarication or lying has infected our culture. Truthfulness is no longer a virtue people try to adopt for their lives. Conversely Masonic Philosophers and our Masonic Ritual of instruction view truth as a divine attribute and as we have previously stated truth should be a the heart of each and every virtue.

Marriage and family are no longer sacred institutions. Infidelity is common place. The work ethics of our forefathers are disappearing from society. Procrastination at the workplace is common with no respect or appreciation given to the job or employment. Society says that it wants respect but modern man's life experiences evidence a serious lack of it. The lack of respect in society is the end result of a lack of purpose, discipline and moral commitment. These are the very ideals that we as Masons, fight to preserve. They are the Cornerstones of our precious Liberties.

VI.   INTEGRITY

A brother whose life evidences qualities of honesty, discipline and courage is proof of a transformed life that has earned respect. His life embodies an individual quest and a determined search for light. It is a fraternal concept shared with our brothers around the world who are of like mind. I submit that the attraction, the spiritual reward, the ultimate objective of our spiritual brotherhood, the character which is the epitome of all virtue is namely "Integrity". In general this quality is defined as our ability to naturally embrace a way of life with moral and ethical principles. It's presence in each of our lives will be the attribute that will continue to draws good men to our lodges.

The driving force of our Masonic Fraternity is to preserve our Liberties by instilling in each of our brothers, the mission to create within each man that knocks at the door of our lodges a thirst for integrity. That desire can only be quenched by a commitment to those moral principles or goals in each of our lives. We must teach that truth, honesty and moral principles are of prime importance. The newly made Brother should be instructed to subsequently understand that a man of integrity is unimpeachable; he is steadfast; his word is his bond. He is never critical of others, even those in which he is in opposition. He restrains his emotions or passions. He is reliable and is one to always satisfy his debts. He stands upon principle no matter what the consequence, whether alone or in a crowd.

The individual struggle for purpose in our lives is found in the attainment of virtue and evidences a larger struggle in the achievement of a moral society. Therefore each brother has a responsibility to himself, as well as society as a whole. Has your Journey to Enlightenment made you free or have we allowed ourselves to wallow in a self destructive complacency? If so, how will this affect our Legacy of Liberty to those closest to us, our families, our Brotherhood and ultimately society? Do we truly live our Masonic philosophy? Are we, you and I, preserving its legacy and willing to fight to defend the principle of liberty that allow each of us unrestricted choice in a disciplined, free society? Our brothers that have completed their labors in this reality have left each of us a legacy, a gift, a true treasure to enrich each of our lives.

From the earliest of time, our Masonic Fraternity has introduced revolutionary concepts which are a reflection of our order's discipline and purpose for our lives. From the equality and respect demanded by the operative brothers of the 13th century to the concepts of democracy fostered within our early lodges, we have boldly elected our own leaders independent of the influences of church or government. These years have seen us foster Human Rights where each man was valued by his character rather than his wealth, and we have with committed determination defended the rights of the worker. The fraternity's influence on the Arts and Architecture, as are our support of Public Education and the health of society, have been identifying landmarks of our Order. All are basic fundamental concepts of a free society as advocated and encouraged by our Spiritual Brotherhood. All of these precious freedoms of our Royal Order of Freemasonry, my Brothers, are in our hands. What will be their destiny?

I thank you, Grand Master, and each of you, my dear brothers, for allowing me the privilege of delivering this paper.

ALBERT PIKE 101
by Arturo de Hoyos, 33°, G.C., PM
Grand Archivist/Grand Historian, Supreme Council, SJUSA

Robert Freke Gould (1836-1915), a founding member and the second Master of Quatuor Coronati Lodge No. 2076 (London) is often touted as England's greatest Masonic historian. Author of *The History of Freemasonry*, his work helped lay the foundation of the 'authentic school' of Masonic research, which looked beyond the traditions of the Craft, and sought factual evidence by which we might discover our origins. Yet his work wasn't perfect. For example, he believed that the English "Antient Grand Lodge" was schismatic, whereas we now know that it was formed by unattached Irish Masons in London. However, when weighed against the enormous amount of factual evidence he uncovered and published, this error is less than a blemish.

No historian is perfect, but every true historian attempts to tell the truth and state facts as clearly and honestly as possible, based upon the evidence at hand. Realizing that the march of human progress stops for no man, we can continue to admire our forefathers, in spite of mistaken notions. In the earliest days of our fraternity, the luminaries of the day promoted the notion that tradition was history. Thus, the *Constitutions of the Free-Masons* (1723), which was the first book published by the premiere Grand Lodge, asserts that Adam was a Mason. We wink and nod at this today, but still bow in respect to the founders who had the vision which created the organization to which we proudly belong.

Of course, all fields of study move forward. Isaac Newton, the father of physics, and one of the greatest geniuses of all time, could never have imagined that some of his works would be eclipsed by Albert Einstein, who himself mistakenly fought against aspects of quantum mechanics (e.g., nonlocality), we know to be true today. In spite of any errors they made, they earned their place in the pantheon of science, and their likenesses justly adorn classrooms (and homes) throughout the world.

In an unblushing statement of admiration, Robert F. Gould stated that Albert Pike (1809-91), "was himself probably the most gifted of all the scholars and antiquaries whose writings have from time to time cast a luster on the literature of Freemasonry" (*Ars Quatuor Coronatorum* 16 [1903], p. 28). This isn't because Pike was perfect, of course. It was because he was an indefatigable researcher with an analytical mind, who collected, edited and published about 5000 pages of historical documents in his *Official Bulletin*, and *dozens* of other works. Gould's brief biography of Pike (*Ars Quatuor Coronatorum*,vol. 4 (1891), pp. 116-57) reveals him to be a person of remarkable insight.

Some of you know that I spent 20 years reverse-engineering Pike's *Morals and Dogma*, and that I published an annotated edition, which includes over 4000 notes, as well as identifies the sources of the text. In my introduction I made no apology for Pike's errors, and I noted them throughout the text. But the works still stands as a remarkably inspiring work, and most of its slips are incidental to the time in which it was produced. They do not materially detract from the value of the book in the least. I stated that "The relevance of *Morals and Dogma* today lies in its exploration of the great questions and philosophical dilemmas which have always moved humanity. Particularly for the Mason, this book serves the useful purpose of putting Masonic morality and ethics within the context of the general society. *Morals and Dogma* bids man to think large—to cast aside the petty concerns of everyday life and to be better than he even believes he can be."

Pike was a participant in the true search for Freemasonry's origins. He wrote, "Even Blue Masonry cannot trace back its authentic history, with its present Degrees, further than the year 1700, if so far" (*Morals and Dogma* 13:15). He believed that he had found evidence of Hermetic influences in Masonic symbolism—something which is still debated today, but accepted by some historians. These arguments are cogently explored in his book *Esoterika: The Symbolism of the Blue Degrees of Freemasonry* (1888), a book praised by both Gould and fellow Masonic historian George W. Speth.

Pike was also interested in anthropology and particularly in the notion of a primitive Aryan race (subjects of his time). His private speculations were gathered and published after his death. The Supreme Council's Archives includes *hundreds* of works by Pike, including his translations of the Hindu Vedas (over 8000 pages).

In the approximately 1900 pages of his last revision of the Scottish Rite rituals his personal ideas regarding the Aryan people are mentioned on only a couple of pages. In their context, this minor error amounts to about the same offense as a Christmas play which names the three wise men Balthasar, Melchior, and Gaspar.

Pike's slips do not demonstrate that he had a mistaken notions regarding Freemasonry's 'dogma' (teachings) or intent. In fact, his definition of Freemasonry, and its purposes is as inspiring today as when it was first written:

"Masonry is a march and a struggle toward the Light. For the individual as well as the nation, Light is Virtue, Manliness, Intelligence, Liberty. Tyranny over the soul or body, is darkness." (*Morals and Dogma* 2:34)

"Above all remember that Masonry is the realm of peace, and that "among Masons there must be no dissension, but only that noble emulation, which can best work and best agree." Wherever there is strife and hatred among the Brethren, there is no Masonry; for Masonry is Peace, and Brotherly Love, and Concord. Masonry is the great Peace Society of the world. Wherever it exists, it struggles to prevent international difficulties and disputes; and to bind Republics, Kingdoms, and Empires together in one great band of peace and amity. It would not so often struggle in vain, if Masons knew their power and valued their oaths." (*Morals and Dogma* 6:20–21)

"Masonry is useful to all men: to the learned, because it affords them the opportunity of exercising their talents upon subjects eminently worthy of their attention; to the illiterate, because it offers them important instruction; to the young, because it presents them with salutary precepts and good examples, and accustoms them to reflect on the proper mode of living; to the man of the world, whom it furnishes with noble and useful recreation; to the traveler, whom it enables to find friends and brothers in countries where else he would be isolated and solitary; to the worthy man in misfortune, to whom it gives assistance; to the afflicted, on whom it lavishes consolation; to the charitable man, whom it enables to do more good, by uniting with those who are charitable like himself; and to all who have souls capable of appreciating its importance, and of enjoying the charms of a friendship founded on the same principles of religion, morality, and philanthropy.

"A Freemason, therefore, should be a man of honor and of conscience, preferring his duty to everything beside, even to his life; independent in his opinions, and of good morals; submissive to the laws, devoted to humanity, to his country, to his family; kind and indulgent to his brethren, friend of all virtuous men, and ready to assist his fellows by all means in his power. Masonry is not made for cold souls and narrow minds, that do not comprehend its lofty mission and sublime apostolate. Here the anathema against lukewarm souls applies.

"To comfort misfortune, to popularize knowledge, to teach whatever is true and pure in religion and philosophy, to accustom men to respect order and the proprieties of life, to point out the way to genuine happiness, to prepare for that fortunate period, when all the factions of the Human Family, united by the bonds of Toleration and Fraternity, shall be but one household—these are labors that may well excite zeal and even enthusiasm." (*Morals and Dogma* 8:8)

"Masonry is the universal morality which is suitable to the inhabitants of every clime, to the man of every creed. It has taught no doctrines, except those truths that tend directly to the well-being of man." (*Morals and Dogma* 10:6)

"Masonry is engaged in her crusade, against ignorance, intolerance, fanaticism, superstition, uncharitableness, and error." (*Morals and Dogma* 15:2)

"Freemasonry is the subjugation of the Human that is in man by the Divine; the Conquest of the Appetites and Passions by the Moral Sense and the Reason; a continual effort, struggle, and warfare of the Spiritual against the Material and Sensual. That victory, when it has been achieved and secured, and the conqueror may rest upon his shield and wear the well-earned laurels, is the true Holy Empire." (*Morals and Dogma* 32:78)

No, Albert Pike was not perfect, and never claimed to be. If you're looking for 'perfection,' look to religious characters. As a 'warts and all' historian, I prefer flawed people—that is, people who accomplish remarkable things in spite of the weakness of the human condition; in spite of errors of judgment; in spite of mistaken views. These are the people who inspire me, because they are people I—as a flawed human being—can understand, and can look up to.

No, Albert Pike was not perfect, but he was faithful to Freemasonry to the end of his life. He discharged his duties, and remained true and faithful to the fraternity. He built up a Masonic system which continues to inspire people around the world, and his works inspire us to be better. I believe the honor we tender him is well-deserved.

To the memory of him who said:

"When I am dead, I wish my monument to be builded only in the hearts and memories of my Brethren of the Ancient and Accepted Scottish Rite, and my name to be remembered by them in every country, no matter what language men may speak there, where the light of the Ancient and Accepted Scottish Rite shall shine, and its oracles of Truth and Wisdom be reverently listened to."

He has lived!

The fruits of his labors live after him.

Take due notice thereof and govern yourselves accordingly.

WHO ARE WE, AND WHERE DO WE STAND
by Robert L. Poll, 32°
Perfect Union Lodge #1

What is Freemasonry? The answer would seem simple: an esoteric fraternity. If you press the question you will most likely be treated to a poetically minded response incorporating words like "brotherhood", "enlightenment", "ancient symbolism" and a history stretching back as far as the eye can see. Freemasons usually think highly of their fraternity and will happily let you know why. The Order certainly does have a prestigious history and its surrounding air of benevolence, mystery, and ancient arts does draw interest. But we still haven't found an answer. All this poetic language is nice, enticing even, but what is Freemasonry? Why does it even exist in the first place? If you pay attention, the most common answer found is "to seek enlightenment."

So we have an answer, Freemasonry exists to show people the door to enlightenment, but what then? How can one attain this very lofty goal? Surely, one cannot find enlightenment like finding a pair of lost socks; so let us look to the leadership for guidance, the masters who have attained the highest ranks of the order. I'm fairly sure that many who look at their leadership will not see the fabled enlightenment, but will almost certainly just see men. So, if the vast majority of masters in Freemasonry are not truly enlightened, but rather just men, then how is one to attain enlightenment in freemasonry?

Maybe we didn't look at the words well enough, "seek enlightenment." Although obscure, the meaning is there, to *"seek."* So are we not expected to find enlightenment, just to seek it? That brings a very abstract goal down to reachable lengths. In fact, this view is better embodied by a different answer, although not one as impressive as "to seek enlightenment."

"To take good men, and make them better." Although one may not see it at first, I believe this best embodies what freemasonry is trying to achieve on many levels. Freemasonry itself is clearly not designed, at least anymore, to create enlightened masters. This may have once been true, and I feel that what draws many to freemasonry is the echoes of the past teachings. It's not unlike gazing at old mossy ruins in the hopes that you might glean some profound insight. When we've simply gazed at the ruins long enough though, all we've really learned is that something was here, and now it's not. Unfortunately, part of this loss (and only a part) is owed to the filter of freemasonry. To maintain the heart of freemasonry a filter among potential candidates is necessary. To maintain the fertility and safety to actually invoke the legendary enlightenment among its members, a far greater filter almost amounting to complete secrecy is necessary, one which freemasonry simply can't muster anymore.

So we come back to the goal of freemasonry, "To take good men, and make them better." The filter most of freemasonry has now is designed, to greater and lesser extents, to let in good men and to keep out troubled or problematic ones. So we've come to where Freemasonry is more or less not designed to create enlightenment among its members, but is, if freemasonry does not deteriorate further, in a position to make good people better. So what then? Are Freemasons supposed to simply sit in lodges and brag about how good they are? Certainly not. The phrase mentioned earlier, "To take good men, and make them better," has more than one level. Once a Freemason has gained all that can be gleaned from the main institution, (regardless if they continue to pursue enlightenment inside other smaller and better equipped institutions) they must impose the phrase, "To take good men, and make them better," onto their environment.

But if that's the ultimate destination of modern Freemasonry, to make a good person better who will then, in turn, make a good place better, why not just cut out the middle man entirely? Why do we need to make a good man better at all? Why not simply cut to the chase and, as an organization, make a good *place* better? Certainly that's what many fine charities attempt to do, and they all make notable impacts in medicine, relief, hunger, and a host of other areas. Why not become a charity? Because the answer is simple, it would be the last nail in our ancient, esoteric coffin.

To "seek enlightenment" is the cornerstone of the original plan of Freemasonry. Members were not content to simply read about mysticism, morality, or any of the other teachings of Masonry. They wholeheartedly pursued these elusive and almost brazenly unattainable concepts. They delved bravely into the heart of metaphysical, theological, and even psychological and scientific debates and ideas. Rather than being satisfied to reach for the attainable, they pursued concepts that we wouldn't dare deliberate today for fear of possible backlash and harsh scrutiny from our fellows. From their esoteric explorations, which were so controversial that they had no choice but to duck away in secrecy for fear of public repercussions, they etched down all we hold dear in Freemasonry. All of our symbols, philosophies, and rituals where the results of deep and profound exploration of the spirit, the nature of our divine origins, regardless of any religion, (which is in actuality, another way of saying *perspective*) and the very concepts of our reality. They delved and reached for depths that we do not, and because of this, the old masters were able to achieve what so deeply confounds us today.

So where do we stand now?

We could take that last step, and become what freemasonry was never designed for in the first place - being a charity. This is not a hard thing to do. In fact, all one really needs to do is nothing. Freemasonry is already leaning in this direction. If we wanted, we could very easily blend into the background until only remembered as a thumbtacked banner saying "Founded in (whatever year)."

Or, we could once again pursue the lavishly impossible - the original goals. The phrase "To take good men, and make them better," has many levels, and it does indeed. How much "better" is entirely up to the individual, but if an initiation is done properly, it can instill this old desire for enlightenment, the drive to learn and seek. This was the whole point of the Masonic initiation, and it was put in place by those far wiser than us today. Some parts even go back long before those who compiled it into what we see now. But it was created with purpose, and it might mean that the steps of the old masters are no longer just a faint fantasy. If our hearts and souls are poured into it, old dusty gears might creak to life and once again inspire this drive in its initiates.

It is possible to turn freemasonry around, but a choice must be made. Which path are we to take? We can't stagnate in the middle; change will happen whether we will it or not, but we can try to guide it like the sail of a ship. Whether into the wind or away, ultimately a deep reflection about who we are and where we want to be is necessary.

IN THE PRESENCE OF FIRE
Various Esoteric Philosophies and Freemasonry
by River Folsom, MM
Livingston Lodge #160

Probing the veil, discerning the trans-mundane, is the highest aspiration of all wise men.

הנהר

Hermeticism is an interesting structure of principles presented as axiomatic propositions to describe and explain various qualities of the universe. The principles are seven in number and specifically mentalism, polarity, vibration, rhythm, gender, correspondence, and cause and effect. Utilizing these principles, we will endeavor to identify the multitude of symbols depicted in the Masonic fraternity. The most forward and interesting are the pillars, long depicted artistically, which have in history made their mark in a wide range of beliefs and practices. Consider the representation below -

Here is a common depiction of the pillars, along with other common masonic symbols set as background to the Kabbalah tree of

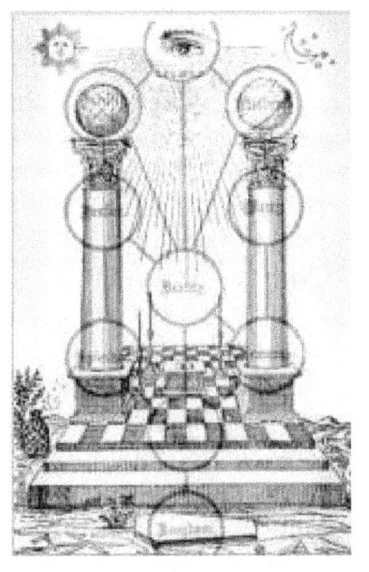

life. The tree, representing ten sephirot and a less common eleventh sephirot breeds a sense of mystery though there are correlations to be noted. Beauty, resting in the middle is the visible balance between the two pillars, notably symbolizing mercy and severity. The tree and artistic depiction also hold a very evident hermetic tie. The sun and moon, white and black, left and right, all the most common physical symbols by which we can attribute polarity; with this difference, that the symbols heavily attribute themselves to gender. Gender, is an extremely important facet of mystic practices and correlates with all other factors in hermeticism along with any 'magick' art and the philosophy there. In explanation, hermeticists have realized that existence is generated and this generation takes on a male and female principle. The two have specific qualities that are not the genital worship so commonly referred to by the less-informed. Masculine properties involve the distribution of organized acts, thoughts, and use of will that in affect pushes the feminine principle, which is generative and cultivating, to produce this "blue-printed" construct. Such things are the talk of high psychology of modern day, that a person may truly change themselves through self-perception, body language, and the like.

The legitimacy of overlaying the tree and masonic board is arguable but supported as individuals of the past have provided common place depictions resembling the same, such as classic Tarot card: II 'The High Priestess.' The suits have an interesting history with this exact form of card being produced in 1910. It had also been stated from Mackey in the *Encyclopedia of Freemasonry* that kabbalah is "connected with the symbolic science of Freemasonry." Other notes involve the higher degree and rites separate from the commons.

This card is of high interest and sheds light on the piece above.

THE HIGH PRIESTESS

The high priestess rests, waxing moon at her feet, Tora in hand, the pillars at her sides, and behind her lies a tapestry or veil decorated with pomegranates and palms. The fruit and leaves of the tapestry are prominent male versus female symbols though the interest and delight is within their arrangement. Three show about her sides, one above, and what would be one roughly behind the cross of her garments, the peak of her seat, and her feet. The waxing moon is common to new developments as it is the beginning of a new cycle for the moon. It is the veil, the depiction on the veil, and the pillars though that grab the most attention to the teachings of Masonic value. Generativity, is the ability of creation, all things are created relatively speaking, and therefore are subject to some form of generation. When imposing mystic things or attempting to discern deity we come to a strange barrier that limits esoteric topics to a small range. Consider this if in doubt, the numerical values of the degree of 33 are long disputed for the relevance to other sources and moral principles. Though it is in Jeremiah {KJV} 33:3 (11 x 3):3 which, being composed of three, always is triune in separation; it is stated "Call unto me, and I will answer thee, and show thee great and mighty things, which thou knowest not." This is an interesting note, as thirty-three is eleven multiplied three times and the eleventh sephirot of the kabalistic tree of life is Da'at or Daath, meaning Knowledge. Knowledge is, like most things under speculation, peculiar in its spiritual value. In genesis of the bible Eve, through temptation, is probed with the desire for knowledge, specifically that of good and evil. Good and evil is a matter of consciousness and debated by the perceptions of the observing individual. This knowledge of such separating qualities taint the human form causing an ejection from paradise. Angels also seem very aware of such things, biblically speaking, yet are not tainted by acknowledgment of the separation, which is strange. It seems to filter down into a very specific explanation which is, the beings above, governed by the will of their creator are not plagued by the acknowledgement of things other than themselves. Human beings however, with free will and passions impressing upon their rationality, are immediately altered by knowledge. For example, if you knew a way to speak a word that causes some personal gain in an unexplainable way it is far more likely that you use it. Though if you knew nothing about such a word and no way of discovering it then you were free from misuse of such a thing. To continue, the priestess has one hand displayed, the left hand, which is resting near the right-hand pillar. This is a curious detail, since the pillar there in Kabbalah is the pillar of mercy and the opposing pillar, severity. In reference to the bible, no character is ever actually referenced as sitting at the left hand of God. It is long stated that Lucifer was the left hand of God yet there is no evidence of this proving it beyond the shadow of a doubt. If it is Lucifer before the fall that sat here it has some very striking implications. A few details will further bring these symbols to light through the use of earlier beliefs such as the Isis and Osiris relationship from the Egyptian mythos. Isis was a wife and sister, being that, she existed with Osiris under similar life spans and the two generated the son, Horus. Vedantic texts also hold allegorical representations of this being the serpent in the void. Further, the three represent Father, Mother, and Son. The bible itself, reinforces the concept that a generative principle existed before man

and before creation in Genesis 1:26 {KJV} "Let us make man in our image," which is elaborated on within the star of David or Hexagram which I will endeavor to explain now for the sake of inspiration.

The star is composed of two triangles facing opposing directions sharing a common center point. The first upward facing triangle is composed from top to right to left as, "Almighty God, Son, and the Holy Spirit" to the opposing as "Father, Mother, Son." If taking a step back to the holy spirit, then I am comfortable assuring it as a representation of the feminine generative quality. This concept of higher trinity to lower trinity is not a revelation by any means. Hermeticism provides what is the most popular axiom "As above, so below. As below, so above" which can be used to describe both physical and mental situations. Physically, it corresponds to inherent similarities between the "here" and "there." It also alludes to a certain form of self-betterment by using higher faculties to naturally alter the lower. Spirit, Soul, and Body from highest to lowest acts as a miraculous example. The finer moralities hidden within the nature of man imposing their doctrines into the mentality of the mortal soul forcing apparent changes upon

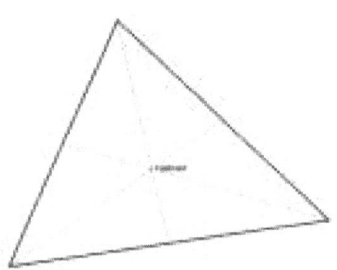
the body; all of which is miraculous by definition. Freemasonry teaches through tools to improve a man, such tools have a physical purpose and a mental one. The powerful use of such tools, being the wise use of knowledge, better molds the man by his own hands than being fashioned by another. Another similar symbol to represent early Gnostic tradition is the center of a triangle with lines between the various points that may easily be explained through some of the deity philosophies before our modern age. Some early concepts involved a God of Good, a God of Evil, and then a High God similar to the explanations above. In addition, there is the formation of a central being or a creator God, a demiurge. As a personal note, it is safe to say that no man may know God as you know God. This statement promotes the idea of personal spiritual relationships, protecting ourselves from egotistical acts from and against others, that we may cooperate on that great journey, the sum of all work in our lives.

Through all these things there is an emphasis on gender. The aspect of gender is symbolic of much higher things which I will begin to dissect. Tarot card: VI "The Lovers" is a good artistic representation of the coming topics.

The card shows a man and a woman standing on equal ground, the female looks on to the apparently divine being above and beyond them while the man looks at the woman across from him. Consider the dual facets of conscious activity, sub(internal) facilities and external cooperating with a host practically unaware of this relationship. This is an important factor since the subconscious mind easily dictates mood and other things presumably out of the control of the receiving individual. Even so, the masculine conscious communicates with the feminine subconscious mind impressing aforementioned "blue-prints" or desires while the feminine begins to generate those desires. The entity above them, seen only by the subconscious, works through the *in total* three step communication process. When attempting to change oneself all acts of progress begin this way, with mental faculties changing perception. This is the practice of sages, manifestation. One of the major factors in Kabbalah from Kether(Knowing) to Malkuth(Kingdom) is the process by which one makes anew in the physical world. To the budding alchemy enthusiast, it is by symbolic chemical process that one burns away counter-productive habits to then solidify the new state of being. Understanding the concept of masculine imposing upon our feminine ability to cultivate is truly one of the earliest "personal" initiations as these teachings are easily considered a science oriented in morality and expanded upon in a progressive manner, step by step the way becomes more clear.

So at this point the wonder may be, why are we talking about gender principles? Earlier I mentioned the manifestation associated with the proper use of these concepts. The greater portion rests within the many theories on the Law of Attraction or the idea that was we govern our mentality and may bring to us what we desire, more easily said, manifest with the mind.

SYMBOLIC INITIATIONS

The concept of initiation is a grand thing with implied acts such as rites, disclosed information, allegiance, and the like. Though what is the initiation presented to mankind that so separates us? In Eden, Eve (feminine) received through Lucifer the first step of knowledge or the acknowledgement of separation in Good against Evil. Have you ever wondered why the name Lucifer means *Light Bringer*? The reason can be argued that such a being could not act without the will of God especially since it is never stated that angelic creatures have free will. In fact, it is more interesting that the "special" quality of a human, biblically speaking, is the power to make decisions that move "toward or away" from the path of our chosen deity.

Baphomet, a word that by its very pronunciation and structure instills worry and wonder is the character the Knights Templar were accused of worshiping under King Philip the IV. This word is assumedly a being or name for an entity but the idea of this is improbable. The word is a construct of three syllables with reference to various principles in other doctrines. To begin, Ba - pho - met is similar to the Egyptian Deities Ba, Phat, and Ma'at (Wife to Thoth) respectively. The words are in rough translation Spirit, Mind, Body along with a deity with a name similar to Phat, notably Ptah or the master craftsman. The word by Latin structure can be seen as *Baphometis* or the baptism in the knowledge of mathematics. The word, syllabled and reversed Ab - ohp - tem are typically seen as a representation of a specific Latin phrase *Templi omnium hominum pacis abhas* or "The God of the temple of Peace among men." This is a curious statement as with little consideration this appears to be a reference to the God of King Solomon's Temple. The depictions of Baphomet being a representation of balance both celestially and in gender also declare a movement between two forms of spiritual travel, the right and left hand path which will be elaborated on later. This depiction though, used by *Eliphas Levi* also acts as a reference to the Hindu lore of the Goat of Mendes. The story short is a farmer that loses his daughter to Shiva. In distaste and rejection has his head removed from his shoulders but in mercy Shiva replaces his head with the head of a goat. The most scholarly opinion though is in the idea that the word was not in use and manufactured much more recently in history. Still forward, the word *Abufihamat*, Arabic for "Father of Wisdom" from

Barrett's *A Brief History of Secret Societies* p. 56 has been accepted as a possible early form of the word from the Man of the Mountain or Sufi Muslims that the Templars would have had contact with in their time.

CONTEMPLATING THE INEFFABLE

Divinity is holding the qualities of the divine which in itself is to be excellent to the state of being God or God-like. It brings up a certain confusion as the word cannot be of immediate use to determine the qualities of Deity. The list can go on with the most popular of a High God or a deity of the chief religions is normally omnipotent, omniscient, omnipresent, and may have complete, some, or absolutely no control over the physical existence depending upon who you talk to. Though deity seems to be other worldly in a sense that it would not be describable by such terms to the mystic or deep believer. The state of single being is easily accepted but from there fragments or lesser deities emerge in the minds of the populace as either other beings or as stated fragments of the original that operate in a specific category which is a part of the Higher. To debate the philosophies would through cyclical logic and personal motivations end in what is most logical - angry ranting. So let us take away the necessity of proving unless it provides since I will not lean toward any particular mode of thought except when writing about a certain mode of thinking, society, or philosophy.

Thoth, *Djehuti*, or the Egyptian deity of writing and knowledge has of most High deities many similarities. The most immediate quality is the mythic conception of the being in that he was self-made, a popular mode of thinking about most of the popular gods today. He represents a certain state of mental welfare and is depicted as Ibis headed. The Ibis seems quite standard other than the animal being sacred to Thoth, but on a side note the Ibis receives its nourishment by using the long beak and prying through muddy lands. The later developments to make this being the "Spiritual Father of Hermeticism" rest in the Thoth - Hermes association. This relationship between the two deities formed an expectation of cultural connection and would later bind Mercurius, the Roman equivalent of Hermes to Thoth. The title of Mercurius is certainly interesting as Mercury in its alchemical significance is easily associated with the mental development, the manner by which one receives information, and the sensory perception in the physical or beyond. The planet Mercury is even considered a major influence upon these factors in Astrology and many individuals attempt to be aware of the times in which the planet is in retrograde as it dilutes the attention. This mythic character symbolizes hermeticism as it is even today a collection of Greek and Egyptian philosophy dated to approximately the second and third century C.E. compounded into axioms to be accepted as methods of discerning the divine and qualities beyond that which we can immediately perceive.

THE ART OF CONVEYING A MESSAGE
by Jonathan K Poll 32°
Perfect Union Lodge #1
Asst. Secretary, Louisiana Lodge of Research

In an old tale, there was a man praying next to a river that led into a nearby town. The radio, which sat next to him, was playing a nice melody when a news report cut in. It spoke of a massive storm coming in that was going to flood the town.

"I am a religious man," he told himself. "I pray. God loves me. He will protect me."

A while later someone came down the river in a row boat. "Hey you! You there by the shore, the town is going to flood. Let me take you to safety."

"I am a religious man," he called back. "I pray. God loves me. He will protect me." Later, when the rain began to fall and the rivers banks began to rise a helicopter flew overhead and a man on a loudspeaker called out. "You there, you by the shore! The town is flooding. Grab this ladder and let us take you to safety.

"I am a religious man," he called back. "I pray. God loves me. He'll protect me." A little while later the man drowned.

When he reached the Gates of Saint Peter, he demanded an audience with the Lord. "Lord," he said, "I am a religious man. I pray. I thought you loved me. How could you let this happen?"

The Lord said, "I sent you a news report, a man in a row boat, and a helicopter. What are you doing here!?"

Stories can weave a tapestry of colorful worlds and fantastic images, and when expressed in the proper manner can convey an idea that strikes at one's very core. A single book can forever shape the imagination of an entire generation and in so doing drastically alter the course a nation is set on. The rituals we work in Freemasonry run far deeper than mere fictions. When conveyed by the right people, on the right person, and in the correct setting, we as Masons are truly able to show our initiates the path towards enlightenment.

The lessons a professor gives during an arduous and mentally exhausting algebra lecture are unlikely to capture the attention of an audience as a super hero, action movie might. However, most will dismiss the action movie as meaningless fluff and will give it very little credence, unlike the teachings of a respected university professor. On the one hand, you have valuable information whose delivery mechanism can't reach mass numbers of people; and on the other you have a seemingly meaningless movie that not only reaches the masses but is deeply ingrained upon their imagination. These movies affect people on a subconscious level. However, they can never go beyond the subconscious because they are perceived as simple action movies and have the public perception of being intellectually worthless. It is a conundrum of trying to be academic and convey an important message while still engaging and impressing the recipient.

One needs to look no further than what lies on top of every Masonic Altar to see how the ancient masters conveyed their wisdom to the masses. The Holy Bible is filled with profound and stirring stories that do indeed shape the imagination. When one looks just beyond the religious aspect, it is also filled with countless moral and social lessons. There are those who accept every word in the Bible as factual, historical, and religious truth. There are likewise Masons who will tell you that every word of the Masonic ritual is factual and historically accurate. We should realize that even if the Bible contained no religious interpretations, and the Masonic ritual contained not a hint of historical references, both would still be filled with profound moral truths. They both teach us to be better. As absurd as it sounds it's not really all that important, for this discussion, if the Bible or Masonic ritual is true at all.

If there was a super hero movie that was fun, engaging and at the same time including lessons of algebra, no one would be able to say that every line of the movie was factual. There is no such thing as people flying around in capes and fighting evil, goateed super villains but that wouldn't mean the movie was valueless. If it was instructing actual lessons of high level mathematics then there would indeed be a lot of content that would be extremely useful and it would be conveyed it in a manner that would hold people's attention. The ancient masters most certainly managed to split the difference by giving vital life lessons in the form of fantastical tales.

For example let's look at the Bible story of Daniel and the lion's den. In the story Daniel, who was a man of deep faith, prayed to God three times a day. Daniel was appointed by the Persian King to be head of a commission. Some wicked men, who very much disliked Daniel, convinced the King to pass a law that people could only pray to the King for thirty days. In that time the wicked men found Daniel praying to his God and reported him to the King. The King very much liked Daniel but could find no way to spare him from the law so he was forced to punish him as the law prescribed by throwing him into a lion's den. The King told Daniel that if he was truly faithful, his God would protect him. The next morning the King went back to the lion's den. He called out to Daniel, and Daniel called back, telling the King that God had shut the mouths of the lions and saved him.

This story is a rather remarkable one. Now in these modern times most pastors would never suggest that it would be safe to go into a lion's den, even for the most faithful. Stepping back, this story does have a deeper underlying message: one of faith, overcoming the wicked, and of devotion. The truth of the story itself, at the end of the day, doesn't really matter. Even if the event happened exactly as written, or if it was a complete fiction, the deeper message and its impact on us is all the same.

The Bible, with its deep symbolic lessons, is the perfect guide for how Freemasonry should teach. The Bible has been a very successful medium to convey a deeper message to countless numbers of people; just as our rituals have been successful in conveying vitally important lessons to our candidates. No person of true faith would tarnish or ridicule the Bible, or any book of sincere faith. With the weight of the solemn nature surrounding the Bible, the symbolic lessons within are received with a greater level of credence. The same principle is applied to our ritual; the message we are trying to convey is amplified exponentially when we impart it in the most solemn of settings, as to impress on the candidate the deep significance of what they are experiencing. When the ritual is delivered with conviction, fluency, and grace of word then it shows the candidate how we as Masons don't just know the words; we live them and have a deep understanding of them.

Let's go back to the analogy of the algebra professor. If in the middle of his lecture he is stumbling over every other word and constantly referring to his text book to tell him what to say next, then the students are going to have very little faith that he understands what he is trying to teach. The lesson as a whole is in danger of being lost on the students. Our ritual is the most powerful tool in Freemasonry; to offer these lessons to candidates is the entire reason for our existence. At the end of the day it doesn't really matter if every word of them are true as that is not the point of the ritual; however, the manner in which they are conveyed, who they are conveyed on, and by whom they are conveyed is of the highest importance. We must always take charge of our sacred duty to shine this light on all initiates. We must always be in search of more knowledge, more light so that we are able to pass along our wisdom to better the next generation. Our journey to obtain more light does not stop in the lodge. Our journey of learning is never over; our path of obtaining more light will go on throughout our whole lifetime.

VIBRATIONS
by Elmo J. Barnes, 32° KCCH
Perfect Union Lodge #1
Director of Work, Valley of New Orleans

What is a Vibration? A vibration is a mechanical phenomenon whereby oscillations occur around an equilibrium point, such as the waves that occur around a finger that is pushed into water. And how does this affect us?

We can look around and vibrations are all around us. We hear because of vibrations. We know this as sound. We see because of vibrations. We know this as sight. All colors coming into our eyes are part of the spectrum of light, which correlates directly to audio by way of a machine known as a spectrometer. For instance, red has a vibratory resonance that is HZ = 126.HZ – 2016 HZ and corresponds to the note of "C". Color is a wave that travels through space and is measured in NANO Meters (NM) which are in the visible spectrum from 380-740 NM.

Everything we see, hear, touch, feel, and maybe even think (as brain waves produce electrical chemical pulses which are vibrations that travel through time and space) are vibrations. We are, ourselves, vibrations. So it is absolutely necessary to produce, and be exposed to, the most harmonious vibrations as possible.

In this article, I will be addressing the musical notes in the vibration range of 432-HZ. The tuning of musical instruments, were very often tuned to 432 HZ until 1953. After that time, the world standards set the pitch of the note "A" at 440 HZ.

Before 1953, one could find tuning forks in A=432 HZ, and even today using standard chromatic tuners, can still be calibrated to A=432 HZ. This has interesting implications. During the rise of the Nazis in Pre WW II Germany, A=440 HZ was the subject of experimentation. It was discovered that A=440 HZ (and the relative notes that make up the octave) made test subjects more aggressive and uneasy as compared to A=432 HZ and its 12 tonal relations. So, what does this "vibration" have to do with humanity?

There have been some incredible studies on vibrations. The recent revelation of gravity waves in the cosmos comes to mind. This was measured by way of two massive black holes coming into close enough proximity to start orbiting each other. This spiraling of these super dense objects creates "Gravitational Waves" in the fabric of space and time. These "waves" or "ripples" are vibrations that go on like ripples in a pond, much like our moon which affects the tides on our own planet. The gravitational vibrations from the proximity of the moon to the earth are responsible for this. Light, which is vibratory in nature, is both a particle and wave. This has many fascinating implications as the famous thought experiment of Erwin Schrödinger's "Live Cat, Dead Cat". In this experiment, subjects would view a box containing a cat. The goal was to explore the sometimes strange results of quantum super-positions. If a viewer noticed a situation in the box that they knew would kill the cat, the cat then would appear dead to them. If they did not notice the condition, the cat would remain alive. No one ever viewed the cat as both alive *and* dead.

We tend to look in awe at these phenomenons in the macrocosm of the Universe. But, to be sure, it applies to the microcosm as well. So the old saying, "as above, so below" is very true here. We humans, and indeed all living and non living things, are subject to the very same laws of nature and physics as a blade of grass or the lowly amoeba.

Besides today's scientists, philosophers, Shamans and the like, we find that antiquity has had many of the most famous and noted thinkers studying these very things; Pythagoras, Newton, and (even more recently) Einstein are but few of the great scholars of all time to find interest in the study of vibrations.

Pythagoras did a considerable amount of work on vibrations. Using the A=432 HZ (which is somewhat known as the "Um" of the Earth). This vibration is universal, as the laws that apply here on earth, apply anywhere in our Universe whether it's one and one equals two, or the laws of motion, or thermodynamics, and all the paradoxes that may arise from them.

Shamans and holy men have for years told of the human aura, and the colors of the human chakras.

RED: at the base of the spine or the note "C" which is in our normal octave range of standard treble clef music (252 HZ); C# (C sharp) = 270HZ; D= 288HZ; D#= 306HZ; E=324HZ; F=360HZ; F#=360HZ; G=378HZ; G#=405HZ; A=32HZ; A#=459HZ; B=486HZ

These notes have higher or lower equivalents according to the octave being played. We, as Masons, are charged with living in peace and harmony with our brethren and indeed, the entire human family. But, as previously stated, harmony on our part touches every tenant of the Universe in which we are a part of.

In the past, since WWII, countries like the US, Soviet Union, China, and I dare say, many more, have researched into the harmony between the tones. Even asymmetrical harmonies have this as there has to be resolution in all tonal or musical compositions, as "Infinity" as in "PI" does not apply here. It repeats every 8 notes, higher or lower.

Some of us (or maybe all of us) have at times said of another "I just don't like him/her", or "I can't stand his/her voice". Could it be that that person's voice is not harmonious to your ear and brain? Usually after some time together, you may find "harmony" that was not visible or audible to you at first. For example, if one's life force vibrates to the note "F" and you meet a person who vibrates to a "G" which is next on the scale of whole notes, you can connect to this person through the "circle of 5th's" and come to asymmetrical harmony and then to "symmetrical" harmony by experiencing the resolution of the union of the two through the circle.

Please note that simple "Sun Sign Astrology" is about as useful to the native as a pocket knife without a blade. Person Centered Astrology is much more intricate, as the planets plus the moon and sun are set in a series of 12 houses as the 12 tones of music and the "Planets" in these houses work much of the way as the circle of 5th's (or 4th's) do when you encounter another with the said symmetry thus composing a composite of the two charts showing the aspects or positive or negative vibrations between two or more of the planets of each. But, that may be a thought for another time and place!

I have worked with sound ("tones") and colors as a "healing" technique and have found it, in most cases, very effective. I have devoted over 20+ years to this study. I am also a musician and have done recordings in A=440HZ, and A=432HZ and have found through "interviews" with listeners, without letting on the difference in the tuning (A=432/A=440), have more so than not, positive affirmations. Is A=432HZ, the sound of the Earth and cosmos? Maybe we need more open and inquiring minds to validate this. I think our Fraternity is an ideal place to start!

Newton developed calculus to explain the mechanical and mathematical universe. I truly believe we are governed by the same physical laws and that math governs the Sun and Moon and even the most distant galaxy in this universe. String theory, which tries to explain the origins of the universe, is based on the premise of vibrating strings of energy. The strings of a guitar vibrate to produce a certain tone. When all strings are vibrating in harmony, we call it a chord. When not, it's just a mess that will give you a headache. Order and chaos, good and bad, good and evil, good chords and bad chords…but the theory that chaos comes from order, and order comes from chaos, means asymmetrical harmony will become harmonious and of course, vice versa. This is the built in paradox of the physical universe.

Long ago, when I was 14 or 15, I got a guitar method book called "Quadraphonic Fingering". This produced some pretty asymmetrical sounds and (the vibrations) made me feel somewhat agitated and irritable when playing them. Of course, the remedy or "cure", was to play something harmonious. Something my brain could wrap itself around and mathematically find an answer to where this stuff was going. Maybe we, as builders, can take these rough, un-shapened stones and process them into harmony! I believe this is the goal of Masonry and of the Universe all through our individual vibrations (symmetrical or asymmetrical) and finding the "note" as Pete Townsend of the "Who" once said, "So pure and easy". Every part of the "temple" in which we labor in the days of our lives is not an external thing. We are all part of its harmony and vibrations as we are the building blocks that will produce the vibrations that will make chaos, or order.

In closing, let me say this was not to be a music theory lesson, nor a lesson in physics; as I am not qualified to be a teacher of either. But, I have found myself immersed in these subjects and disciplines and speak only as a student. I sincerely hope you will find a spark of interest in these fascinating subjects and search and explore for yourselves. I'll leave you with this old Buddhist proverb; "A humming bird beating its wings, affects the whole world"……Sounds like vibrations to me!

WHY THE FC DEGREE
by J. Quincy Gotte, 32°
Worshipful Master, Rudolph Krause Lodge #433
Treasurer, Valley of Lake Charles, LA

It is difficult to appreciate the FC Degree to its full potential considering the amount of time most of us have spent studying its teachings. There is so much beauty and symbolism in the FC Degree that most of us have missed while seeking more Light. I think it is safe to say that the reason this Degree particularly gets overlooked is because most are looking forward to the Light provided in the MM Degree. With that being said, a large portion of Light in the FC Degree becomes hidden in shadows. But we would do well to understand that the teachings of the FC Degree are crucial to our development towards becoming a MM.

As I have previously given my personal opinion around what the EA Degree means to me, I will attempt to do the same in my thoughts around the FC Degree. As in the EA Degree, there is no way to communicate the full scope of this Degree with 1500 words or less; nor could I possibly pretend that there are no other applications or interpretations that are cherished and relevant to the journey of so many other Brothers. This is but one of many points of view. So as with the EA Degree, I would like to touch on only a few areas that have had an effect on my journey as a FC of Freemasonry.

BEFORE THE FC, WE MUST REASON FOR THE LEFT IN THE EA DEGREE

We may understand the tools of the EA and their significance to be the tools used to discipline or shape and rule our base nature, desires, and passions. *Albert Pike's "Morals & Dogma"* opens the EA with *"Force, unregulated or ill-regulated"*, then it goes on with a poetic description of blind force, then it goes on to conclude *"is destruction and ruin"*. We can read many stories where good men allowed their passions to bring about misfortune. The story of Cain and Abel (G-D did commune with Cain), is one in particular that tells of such; there is also the story of Jacob and Esau. In both stories, we read of strife and injury between brothers at odds, and men who make a decision/or series of decisions of poor judgement based on their passions. It is safe to conclude that we are to bring this force under a disciplined rule.

Some Kabbalistic teachings *("Shaar Hagilgulim" The teachings of Rabbi Isaac Luria translated by Rabbi Chaim Vital)* relate the left shoulder to that of the root of Cain, and the left heel seems to represent the partzuf (form or face) of the Nukveh (the feminine aspect of the Tree of Life) of Asiyah (the world of action), or the Sephirah of Malchut (considered as Kingdom or Bride, which may also represent the final "Heh" or the feminine aspect of the Tetragrammaton, as well as this corporeal realm we live in). Also, *Chayyim Vital's Introduction to the Kabbalah of Isaac Luria "The Tree of Life"* teaches that the 3 columns of the Tree of Life, which support the Sephirot, are represented by Abraham as the right column, Jacob as the middle column, and Isaac as the left column.

The right column of the Tree of Life symbol represents Loving Kindness and Mercy, which reflects the thoughtfulness and selflessness of Abraham; the middle column represents Truth, or the court, which reflects truth given to Jacob (Micah 7:20) which balances the Left & Right; the left column represents Harsh Judgement, which reflects the binding of Isaac on the altar. *"Gates of Light" Rabbi Joseph Gikatilla*

We can see time and again the symbolism of the left and the right throughout the teachings of Kabbalah, which are evident within the teachings of Freemasonry. The left shoulder being the limb closest to the heart is a fitting symbol of our actions driven by our passions. The sharp piercing experienced, and the *"knlg"* of the *"le ke"* may serve as a reflection of the importance of the submission of those attributes before we can go further in our quest for more Light.

I only mention this to elevate the significance of the "left" in the EA Degree. So, once we have brought our passions and base nature under the strengthened disciplines *("t le hd plr tt std on t ph o Kg Smn's Tp")* learned in the EA Degree, we are able to pass to the Degree of FC and establish our Faith on a new level with a mindset ready to receive -not for self-gratification alone, but for the ultimate sake of bestowing, which reflects the "right" attribute of Mercy and Loving Kindness. But before we can bestow Mercy and Loving Kindness, there is a progressive ascension that needs to be undertaken.

THE SIGNIFICANCE OF THE RIGHT IN THE FC

"Reason is far from being the only guide, in morals or in political science. Love or loving-kindness must keep it company..." "We must also have faith in ourselves, and in our fellows and people..." "We must not listen to Reason alone. Force comes more from Faith and Love..." "Albert Pike's Morals & Dogma- Annotated Edition" -De Hoyos

After the explanation of the Pillars **** & ******, we must ascend up a winding staircase leading us to the door of the *"Mdl Cmr o Kng Smn's Tp"*, which is found in the right side of the house. As mentioned previously concerning the Left shoulder representing Cain, in that same text the relation to the Right shoulder is that of Abel, which Seth replaced Abel and was first to call upon the Name of G-d. We can also find a concept in *Aryeh Kaplan's "Sefer Yetzirah"* that associates the right foot with thought. It is with this foot that one enters the Temple, and which we progress up the staircase to the *"Mdl Cmr"*, which holds a Spiritual significance.

Before approaching the door to the entrance of the *"Mdl Cmr"*, we are encouraged to become enlightened through the understanding of our Natural World taught through the Seven Liberal Arts and Sciences. For me, this is alluding to the need to become enlightened through Philosophical study and thought; which in ancient times Philosophy consisted of both science and religion or Faith. These teachings were conveyed using symbolism. This is where our strength is tested prior to our coveted establishment within this Degree.

THE ESTABLISHING

It is no common or weak desire to be in a situation where one's views, actions, and core beliefs are to be tried and challenged. Before one can approach this task, one must be well established within his own Faith; and to be well established in one's Faith, one must be familiar with the "natural scriptures" laid out for all to read and learn from. One should understand that establishing a stronger Faith consists of both corporeal and spiritual knowledge.

Imagine believing the earth is flat and then hearing for the first time the concept of it being round, and that the earth is not the center of the universe as you were taught. Great men were put to death and imprisoned for speaking such "heresy" during that time; and now we know these things to be true and common knowledge only after society gave consideration to the possibility. Imagine if you were to close your mind and not give consideration to these facts today; you would be ridiculed and viewed as a fool.

To open the mind to entertain or discover new and different points of view, or to learn something that we typically wouldn't take interest in, is how we approach a consciousness shift needed to receive more Light. We must understand that knowledge is as plentiful as a Cornucopia, waiting for us to feed from; knowledge that ought to be desired and sought after. We must *contend* with, and *establish* this fact prior to our entrance; otherwise, we will not see the complete scope of Light provided, and be in danger of not receiving the full measure of Light in the next Degree because we were not fully prepared by the FC Degree.

THE VISION OF THE PLUMB LINE "AMOS 7:7-8"

The Book of Amos is a woeful book which speaks of impending doom to Israel, but a Blessing to come if they seek after G-d, and turn from the wrong path. Amos is shown a vision of a Plumb Line in the hand of G-d that was set against a wall built true to Plumb. Amos is then told that Israel will not be spared destruction. The vision after this is one of a Basket of Ripe Fruit, and is explained that the evil Israel has committed has matured. Earlier it is explained that judgement comes because Israel is considered to be the chosen people, so they are held to a higher standard. When considering the full scope of the book, the Plumb Line for me is a symbol reflecting a higher standard, as well as the call to a consciousness shift.

ONE OF THE WORKING TOOLS OF OUR PROFESSION

So there is only one tool presented in this Degree that is literally applied directly towards ourselves which we may utilize in this consciousness shift. You remember it to be applied in the same area where the *"Mdl Cmr"* is placed in the house. It is presented for a reason that is important enough to be symbolized in four ways throughout the Degree. It is so relevant that the Pythagorean Theorem known as Euclid's 47th Problem girds our loins as a constant reminder of the need for a consciousness shift throughout our time as a FC. This Degree focuses on cultivating the mind, just as you would plow a field to harvest a crop so there will be *plenty* of provisions for nourishment, joy, and refreshment.

THE CONSCIOUSNESS SHIFT

The 90° angle represents the 1/4 of a circle. The circle is a symbol with many meanings; for this point of view it represents correction completed through a cyclical motion. This alludes to a call for a change of course on four different levels, or cycles, within us in order to obtain correction. If you were to set out on a course in a straight line, and were to apply a 360° turn, you will ultimately not change your course. If you were to set out on a course in a straight line and apply a 90° turn you will change your course within that line but not reach completion. You would need to perform four 90° turns to complete a perfect circle, but ultimately you would not have changed your course, you would only wallow in the labyrinth of your own mind on a single level.

If we are to employ the Kabbalistic concept of the 4 worlds (or levels of thought, dimensions, etc..), which would represent Emanation, Creation, Formation, and Action; and were to set these 4 worlds as 4 different aspects within ourselves, we could apply a 90° angle on 4 different levels of self, and progress up the Spiral Staircase concluding a perfect 360° Circle prior to entering the *"Mdl Cmr"*.

This sounds a lot like a bunch of metaphysical mumbo jumbo at first glance. But let's not confuse the symbolism as a tangible thing. It is not tangible because it is dealing with the will, spirit, and mind. It only becomes tangible through our actions, and is only noticeable if our actions become Higher and Truer than at the start of this Degree. After all, the *La Masonic Monitor* tells us that *"the lessons taught us, as we ascend, should impress upon the mind of every Freemason the importance of discipline, as well as knowledge of natural, mathematical, and metaphysical science."* Only then can we receive our wages as a FC of Freemasonry.

THE WAGES OF A FC

The wages of a FC are ****, ****, and ***. These three have something very similar in common. They are all products of the intellect and skill that is involved in refining them to the state that they are in once we receive them. They are the product of our labor, which we benefit from when we have earned them. The wages themselves are a result of a metaphysical change brought on through the course of perception, creativity, ingenuity, and a skill set on a course to achieve a renewed tangible outcome.

"Every truly intelligent man and woman who is working to spread light in the world is Christ-end, or Light-end, by the actual labor which he or she is seeking to perform. The fact that light partakes of the natures of both G-d and the earth is proved by the names given to the personifications of this light for at one time they are called the "Sons

of Men" and at another time the *"Sons of G-d."* ~ Manly P Hall - *"Melchizedek and the Mystery of Fire"*

So this is why, as a FC, we must try ourselves by the tool of our profession, and stay the course in seeking knowledge and building upon our Faith. The wages received after this consciousness shift will provide nourishment, joy, and refreshment enough to sustain yourself as well as others around you.

THE NEW ORLEANS ROOTS OF FREEMASONRY IN MOBILE, ALABAMA

by Wayne E. Sirmon, 33°
Past Master, Mobile Masonic Lodge No. 40, F&AM of Alabama
Past Master, Texas Lodge of Research

From the earliest days of the French efforts to colonize the central gulf coast, the histories of Mobile, Alabama and New Orleans have been intertwined. Pierre Le Moyne d'Iberville was commissioned by France to "reconnoiter the mouth of the Mississippi and fortify the entrance to it."[1] He first arrived in Pensacola Bay in late 1698 and finding it occupied by the Spanish, he moved west to the mouth of Mobile Bay and explored Dauphin Island before continuing on to coastal Mississippi. In the fall of 1701 he directed his brother Jean Baptiste Le Moyne de Bienville to establish Mobile. While several earlier French outposts had been established, Mobile would be the first colonizing effort to produce a lasting result. Among these initial forts were Ft. Maurepas (1699) on the northern shore of Biloxi Bay, Mississippi and Fort De La Boulaye, (1700) located on the Mississippi River approximately thirty-five miles below New Orleans.[2]

Late in 1701, French forces were shifted from Ft. Maurepas to establish a presence in the Mobile Bay area. The first construction was a warehouse on Massacre Island (now know as Dauphin Island, Alabama). By January 5, 1702, Bienville had recovered from a "late summer epidemic" and left Ft. Maurepas with a small fleet moving supplies to Massacre Island.[3]

Initially established as an Indian trading post at Twenty-three Mile Bluff, Mobile was literally moved downstream to its present location in 1711 when in early summer the residents of "Old Mobile" disassembled the buildings and had the timbers conveyed by floats down the river, where the buildings were reassembled around Ft. Louis according to the city plan developed by Bienville.[4]

Sixteen years after establishing Mobile, Bienville directed the founding of La Nouvelle-Orléans. The capital of French Louisiana shifted from Mobile to Biloxi and finally in 1823 to New Orleans. The region would not come under British control until 1763 at the end of the French and Indian (or Seven Years') War. At the same time, New Orleans, being on the west side of the Mississippi would fall under Spanish rule until 1801 when for a brief time it reverted to French control until the 1803 Louisiana Purchase. Both cities were trading centers far from the seats of national power, and therefore developed interesting, international outlooks on commerce.

The early days of Freemasonry in Louisiana is a complex story and is beyond the scope of this study however the following can be stated without controversy. On April 8, 1812 Louisiana was admitted as eighteenth state of the United States of America. During the colonial and territorial periods, twelve lodges had been established. By the time of statehood, seven lodges bearing allegiance to three Grand Lodges remained. Perfect Union Lodge drew together representatives of these lodges on April 18, 1812 to consider the creation of the Grand Lodge of Louisiana. Five Lodges participated in meetings on May 16 and June 13. The Grand Lodge of Louisiana was established on June 20, 1812.[5]

A group of Masons residing in Mobile received a charter from the newly formed Grand Lodge of Louisiana and on September 4, 1813 Friendship Lodge No. 6 began its labor. The petition to establish the first lodge in south Alabama was signed by: James Lyon, S. H. Garrow, C. Strong Stewart, Dominique Salles, Ed. J. Hazlewood, A. S. Sands, Nathaniel Charles and Samuel Acre.[6] The initial officers were: James Lyon as Worshipful Master; S. H. Garrow as Senior Warden and Charles Stewart as Junior Warden.[7] Lyon published the first newspaper in Mobile, *The Mobile Gazette*. Samuel Garrow would later serve as Mayor from 1824-27 and 1829-31. Since Garrow moved to Mobile from New Orleans, where he "commanded one of the gunboats at the battle of New Orleans", the current assumption is that his Masonic connections in that city led to the request for dispensation for Louisiana to create Friendship Lodge. Other members of Friendship Lodge were John Johnson, Miguel D. Eslava, Frederick Sheffield, Silas Wescott, Thomas C. Newbold and Joseph Krebs.[8] *The Mobile Gazette* printed several items of a Masonic nature during 1819. The first is a notice of a funeral which included "Masonic honors." Another was the announcement of the celebration of St. John the Baptist which was to convene on June 24, 1819.[9]

At that time, the area around Mobile was part of the Mississippi Territory. In 1817, Mississippi received statehood and the eastern part of that Territory was renamed the Alabama Territory. The second lodge in coastal Alabama received a Louisiana charter during this period. Eureka Lodge No. 16 was chartered on July 12, 1819. This Lodge was located at Blakeley which was at the time a rapidly growing port on the eastern shore of Mobile Bay. The charter officers were: W.M. William Coolidge, S.W. Sylvester Bell, and J.W. E. G. Sheffield.[10]

Mobile prospered under American rule and she was admitted into the union on December 14, 1819. The third of Alabama's Louisiana Lodges received her charter on July 12, 1821. On that date Mobile Lodge No. 22 became the final Louisiana Lodge to be established in what was soon to become the state of Alabama. Very little is known about this lodge. It does not even rate a mention in the Oliver Day Street or Joseph Jackson histories of Freemasonry in Alabama. Jordon's *Let There Be Light* only states that "... on July 12, 1821, Mobile No. 22 was chartered at Mobile. Eureka No. 16 became extinct while Mobile No. 22 forfeited its charter."[11]

A communication from the Grand Lodge of Louisiana was read at the December 1824 session of the Grand Lodge of Alabama "charging Mobile Lodge No. 10, with working under their jurisdiction as well as under the jurisdiction of this Grand Loge, and refusing to pay its dues to the said Grand Lodge of Louisiana." The letter was referred to a special committee which reported the next day and offered a lengthy report (see Appendix I). They reported that in 1821 an application was made by Mobile

Lodge to the Grand Lodge of Louisiana for a Charter. A warrant was issued by "one of the Deputy Grand Masters of Louisiana then residing at Blakeley" with the condition that Mobile Lodge must pledge not to admit any member who had been attached to Friendship Lodge No. 6. Due to this requirement the lodge voted to reject the Louisiana charter. The committee then urged those members of Mobile Lodge who were in arrears for dues not paid when they were members of Friendship Lodge No. 6 to settle their accounts with the Grand Lodge of Louisiana.[12]

Later in that same Grand Lodge session a resolution was adopted that directed Mobile Lodge No. 10 to compel any present members to pay any dues in arrears to the Grand Lodge of Louisiana (see Appendix II). The matter appears to have been settled as there are no further references to the matter in the Grand Lodge Proceedings. In October 1827 a fire destroyed the majority of Mobile's business district including the Masonic Hall along with all of the lodge's records. The Grand Lodge of Alabama voted to exempt the lodge from paying dues that year because the lodge sustaining "this heavy loss, will be compelled to make heavy pecuniary disbursements to refit a Lodge Room."[13]

During the cotton boom of the late 1850s, Mobile experienced a transformation from a quiet, minor port to a significant exporter of cotton. The local Masonic community grew and in 1860 the first effort was made to bring the Scottish Rite to Mobile. A group of Master Masons residing in Mobile contacted James C. Batchelor who traveled to Mobile in January, 1860. This group then traveled to New Orleans and received a portion of the higher degrees with a hope of establishing Scottish Rite Masonry in Mobile. The turmoil and civil unrest of the period resulted in no further action being taken to organize the Rite in Mobile until the end of the Civil War.[14]

The effort was renewed during reconstruction when James C. Batchelor and Samuel M. Todd communicated the degrees to a group of Masons in Mobile. The Mobile Valley history indicates that this occurred on December 21, 1867 and that a Lodge of Perfection, Council of Princes of Jerusalem and

Chapter of Rose Croix were established. The list of nineteen Charter Members includes Henry John Shields, 33° and R. F. Knott, 32°, Deputy for Alabama.[15] Other sources differ in details. Lobingier reports from Pike's comments at the Supreme Council session of 1868 that "Ill∴ Bros∴ Batchelor and Todd have planted the Rite in Mobile, under the best auspices..." he later reports that Batchelor organized Mobile Council No. 1 of the Princes of Jerusalem in December, 1867.[16] Carter indicates that two or more bodies were formed in Mobile through the use of the phrase "Bachelor and Todd had established bodies in Mobile, Alabama." 17 Gould's entry refers to "The 1872 Transactions of the Supreme Council show Mobile Lodge of Perfection, No. 1, with thirtyseven members; Mobile Council of Princes of Jerusalem, No. 1, with fifteen members; Mobile Chapter, Knights of Rose Croix, No. 1, with ten members; and Mobile Council of Kadosh, No. 1, with eleven members. These were the earliest bodies of the Rite to be established in the State."[18]

The post-war economy made expansion of the Scottish Rite virtually impossible across the old Confederacy. The Panic of 1874 was a world-wide economic depression that lasted for five years in the United States. While the Panic weakened the national economy, the southern response of retrenchment put many Scottish Rite bodies in an impossible situation. By the 1874 Supreme Council session, Mobile along with Savannah, Richmond, Baltimore, Arkansas, Tennessee and Nebraska were characterized as "dormant." Inspector General Frederick Webber of Kentucky reported observations which echoed by other Inspectors General when he stated that:

Money is scarce and men won't indulge in the Masonic luxury of our Rite. Opposition to the Rite is strong among prominent Masons. Delays between the degrees of the Scottish Rite "often keep out good men." The great expense of furnishing rooms deters the small town from undertaking the formation of the Bodies. It is claimed as an impossibility to commit the work to memory, there is so much of it.[19]

Faced with seemingly unbreachable barriers, the Mobile Masons could not meet their financial obligations and in 1870 the charters were revoked. Mobile would have to wait until the dawn of the twentieth century before the Scottish Rite of Freemasonry would become a permanent part of the Mobile Masonic community.

One explanation for the willingness of Batchelor and Todd to devote such energy to the attempt to establish the Scottish Rite in Mobile is they were first Alabama Masons. James Cunningham Batchelor received his Blue Lodge degrees in Eureka Lodge No. 64 in Greenville, Alabama in 1846. At that time, the twenty-six year old graduate of the Cincinnati Medical College was practicing medicine. In 1853, he would relocate to New Orleans, marry and become increasingly involved in the hierarchy of Freemasonry. His twenty-one year tenure as Grand Secretary began in 1867. Receiving the Fourth through Thirty-second Degrees in 1856, it would take only one year to be elected for the Thirty-third Degree and after only three years as a Scottish Rite Mason, Batchelor would become an Active Member of the Supreme Council. For thirteen years he would serve as Albert Pike's Lieutenant Grand Commander, and after Pike's death in 1891 he would be elected as Grand Commander "for life." His brief time as head of the Supreme Council would end with his death on July 28, 1893. While he is generally considered a Louisianan, he lived from early childhood to his mid thirties as an Alabamian. It would be only natural that he would wish to share his beloved Scottish Rite with the Masons of the state where he grew to manhood.[20]

Samuel Manning Todd became a Mason in Howard Lodge No. 69 in Mobile, being initiated on December 2, 1846 and receiving the Master Mason Degree in February, 1848. Within a year of becoming a Mason, he received the York Rite Chapter and Council degrees in Mobile. After moving to New Orleans he served as Master of Marion Lodge No. 68. This was the same lodge that Albert Pike was affiliated with between 1858 and 1860. John Quincy Adams Fellows, who was elected as an

Active Member of the Supreme Council in 1870, was also a member of Marion Lodge from 1851 until its consolidation with Perfect Union in 1886.[21]

Born near Utica, New York, the family moved south when Todd was "quite young." While it is unsure when he moved from Mobile to New Orleans, it would have been between 1851 and 1855. He is not listed as an officer or member of Marion Lodge in the *Proceeding of 1851*,[22] but by February 22, 1855 he is marching as the First Lieutenant of the Continental Guards militia company.[23] In 1839, he would serve the first of five terms as Grand Master. During the Civil War years he served as Grand Secretary. He first appeared on the Tableau of the Supreme Council in 1868 and served until his death in 1905. While his early efforts to establish the Scottish Rite in Mobile were not successful, he did live to see the chartering of the Mobile Lodge of Perfection and Chapter of Rose Croix.

For ninety days in 1810 an effort was made to unite the people of the central gulf coast into a political force. The Republic of West Florida failed as an idea and rarely appears in our history except as a footnote which references the development of the flag of Texas or a jaunty tune expressing southern sympathies during the rebellions years of the 1860s. However, the boundaries of that almost imaginary country indicate that the pasts and futures of the people who inhabit our coastal plains are bound by history in ways that those who populate the northern portions of our states have yet to understand. *Laissez les bon temps rouler!*

APPENDIX I [24]
Report of Special Committee of the Grand Lodge of Alabama
Eldridge S. Greening (chairman), Daniel Uquhart, William B. Martin
December 18, 1824

Brother Greening from the committee to who was referred the communications from the Grand Lodge of Louisiana, on the subject of Mobile lodge No. 10, held in the city or Mobile, made the following report, which was concurred in by the Grand Lodge:

That they have devoted much attention to the subject matter of the communications as they are entitled to from the elevated sources from which they emanated. A correct explanation of the facts will remove all suspicions of improper conduct on the par of Mobile lodge as a body, and your committee believe that the Grand Lodge of the state of Louisiana have acted under an influence of erroneous impressions as to the existence of the facts in the communication transmitted to this Grand Lodge. From the short space of time allowed your committee, they have been compelled to resort to such testimony only as was immediately in their reach, which consists of a statement of facts submitted to their consideration by the then Worshipful Master elect of Mobile lodge. It may not be improper to observe that entire reliance may be allowed to the credibility of this evidence.

From this statement it appears that in the year 1821, an application was made by Mobile lodge to the Grand Lodge of the state of Louisiana for a Charter, and the sum of seventy or seventy-five dollars transmitted for the purpose of defraying such expenses as might be incident to the issuing of the warrant.

In accordance with the wishes of Mobile lodge a warrant was transmitted to one of the Deputy Grand Masters of Louisiana, then residing at Blakeley. Fettered, however, with a condition that it should not be delivered until Mobile lodge would pledge itself to withhold the privilege of membership to such persons as had previously been attached to Friendship lodge No. 6, and which had previously expired. So soon as this information was communicated to the members elect, the individuals who were about forming Mobile lodge, were called together with a view of ascertaining the sentiments of the lodge, as to the terms upon which they should accept the Charter.

In obedience to the vote of the lodge the Charter was rejected, and your committee feel themselves justified in saying that Mobile lodge No. 10, at no period recognized the claim attempted to be set up over it by the Grand Lodge of the state of Louisiana.

On the contrary, Mobile lodge has at all times since the organization of this Grand Lodge, acknowledged the jurisdiction of this Grand Lodge over it.

Your committee have been informed that some of the members of Mobile lodge are still in arrears to the Grand Lodge of Louisiana, which accrued while they were members of Friendship lodge No. 6, and those feelings of fraternal affection which every principle of our order are calculated to inculcate, induce your committee to recommend that suitable measures should be adopted by this Grand Lodge to coerce a settlement between the defaulting members of Mobile lodge and the Grand Lodge.

From these statements of facts, your committee are satisfied that no circumstance has transpired in relation to the subject matter of the communications which should induce this Grand Loge to withdraw its confidence from Mobile lodge; upon the contrary, your committee encourage a belief that this explanation will be amply sufficient to restore, between the Grand Lodge of Louisiana and Mobile lodge, those feelings of friendship and amity that should ever characterize the brethren of the Mystic Order.

E. S. GREENING, Chairman

APPENDIX II [25]
Resolution of the Grand Lodge of Alabama
December 18, 1824

On motion of brother Uquhart, the following resolution was adopted:

Resolved, that Mobile lodge No. 10, be respectfully requested diligently to inquire whether any of its present members have ever been members of the late Friendship lodge No. 6, and if any such be found, that said lodge No. 10 be requested to ascertain whether they are yet in arrears to the late Friendship lodge No. 6, chartered by the Grand Lodge of the state of Louisiana; and if so, how much, and compel said members to pay up said dues; and that the said lodge No. 10, transmit the amount so collected to the Grand Lodge of Louisiana.

Resolved, that a copy of the foregoing resolution be forwarded by the Grand Secretary to Mobile lodge No. 10 and to the Grand Lodge of the state of Louisiana.

NOTES

1. Jay Higginbotham, "Discovery, Exploration, and Colonization of Mobile Bay to 1711," in *Mobile: the new history of Alabama's first city*, ed. Michael V. R. Thomason (Tuscaloosa: University of Alabama Press, 2001), 16.
2. "Category:French Colonial Forts" *FortWiki*, http://fortwiki.com/Category:French_Colonial_Forts (accessed December 24, 2015).[2]3. Jay Higginbotham, *Old Mobile: Fort Louis de la Louisiane, 1702-1711* (Tuscaloosa: University of Alabama Press, 1977), 29
4. Ibid., 458-459.
5. H. Glenn Jordan, *Let There Be Light, A History of Freemasonry in Louisiana 1763-1989* (Baton Rouge: Bourque Printing, 1990), 9-11.
6. Grand Lodge of Alabama, *Proceedings of the M. W. Grand Lodge of Ancient Free and Accepted Masons of the State of Alabama 1821-1839* (Montgomery: Rogers Printing, 1906), 4.
7. Oliver Day Street, "Historical Sketch of Freemasonry in Alabama," in *Masonic Manual, Grand Lodge A.F. and A. M. of Alabama* (Birmingham: Premier Printing, 1940), 399.
8. Joseph A. Jackson, *Masonry In Alabama: A Sesquicentennial History 1821-1971* (Montgomery: Brown Printing Company, 1970), 29.
9. *Mobile Gazette and Commercial Advertiser*, June 2, 1819.
10. Grand Lodge of Alabama, (introduction) 4.
11. H. Glenn Jordan, 77.
12. Grand Lodge of Alabama, (1824 session) 89-92.
13. Ibid., (1827 session) 183.
14. "The Mobile Scottish Rite; A Brief History" in *Scottish Rite Temple Golden Anniversary Souvenir Program* (Mobile, AL: Commercial Printing Company, 1972), 4.
15. Ibid., 4, 42.
16. Charles S. Lobinger, *The Supreme Council, 33° Mother Council of the World Ancient and Accepted Scottish Rite of Freemasonry, Southern Jurisdiction, U. S. A.* (Louisville, KY: The Standard Printing Co., 1931), 302, 439.

17. James D. Carter, *History of the Supreme Council, 33° (Mother Council of the World) Ancient and Accepted Scottish Rite of Freemasonry Southern Jurisdiction, U.S.A. 1861-1891* (Washington, DC: The Roberts Publishing Company, 1967), 26.
18. Oliver Day Street, "Freemasonry in Alabama" in Dudley Wright, Ed., *Gould's History Of Freemasonry Throughout The World Volume V* (New York NY: Charles Scribner's Sons, 1936), 15.
19. James D. Carter, 84, 90.
20. Charles S. Lobinger, 191-193.
21. Charles S. Lobinger, p. 289-290; James A. Marples, "Albert Pike's Masonic, Templar, And Rosicrucian Record" http://www.masonic.benemerito.net/msricf/papers/marples/marples-AlbertPikeMasonicRecord.pdf accessed May 20, 2011 ; William J. Mollere, "The Development Of Scottish Rite And Its Leadership In Louisiana Freemasonry," presented at the Louisiana Lodge of Research August 15, 1998, Shreveport, LA
22. Grand Lodge of Louisiana, *Proceedings of the M. W. Grand Lodge of Free and Accepted Masons of the State of Louisiana From 22d June 5851 to February 25th 5851* (New Orleans LA: J. L. Sollee, 1851), 20-21.
23. Edward C. Wharton, *A History of the Proceeding in the city of New Orleans, on the occasion of the Funeral Ceremonies in honor of James Abram Garfield, late president of the United States, Which Took Place on Monday, September 26th, 1881* (New Orleans LA: A. W. Hyatt, 1881), 165-166.
24. Grand Lodge of Alabama, (1824 session), 90-92.
25. Ibid., (1824 session), 95.

EARLY GRAND LODGE OF LOUISIANA PROCEEDINGS
(Part One)
by Michael R. Poll, PM
Secretary, Louisiana Lodge of Research

Jokes are often made about the cranky, old Past Master saying something along the lines of, "We didn't do it *that* way in my day!" While comments like these can sometimes be attributed to sour grapes at no longer being in the "seat of authority," there is some truth to such statements. Time *does* bring about change. Masonry changes just as every aspect of life changes. If we were able to somehow go back in time and visit a very early lodge under the Grand Lodge of Louisiana, it is doubtful that we would recognize much of what we saw or heard. Our Masonry has changed that much since its early days. We can debate all day as to if this is good or bad, but it is simply a fact. We don't "do it" the way we use to "do it."

What follows is a rare look at the early days of Louisiana Freemasonry. In 2013, the Louisiana Lodge of Research published, as a bonus book, part one of *The Civil War Years, Proceedings of the Grand Lodge of Louisiana 1861-1862*. Hopefully, we will be able to publish part two (1863-1864) in the next year or two. In 2014, we were lucky enough to be able to publish the "lost" 1812 *Proceedings of the Grand Lodge of Louisiana* in the LLR Transactions. This year, we are publishing all other available Proceedings up until 1830. The early Proceedings which I have been able to locate (after nearly 30 years of sometimes frustrating searching) are: 1818, 1820, 21, 22, 23, 24, 25, 26, 27, 28 & 1830. Many times I was only able to locate discolored and hard to read poor quality photocopies. These Proceedings are published here after being digitally cleaned and restored as best as possible. In the 2016 Transactions, we hope to publish all available Proceedings from 1830 to 1850. After 1850, the Grand Lodge seems to have a full and complete collection of Proceedings.

Why so many of the important Grand Lodge Proceedings prior to 1850 were "lost" is a matter open for debate. It does seem clear, however, that there was a strong desire to change how things were done and an equal desire to forget the past. In my opinion, knowing the past is the only way to be certain of what we want out of the future.

Several things about the Proceedings should be noted. The early Grand Lodge of Louisiana worked in the French language. These Proceedings, however, are published in English. The reason why they are in English seems simple. No other Grand Lodge in the United States worked in any language other than English. The early Grand Lodge of Louisiana published the Proceedings of each year in both French and English because they wanted others to know of the activities of the Grand Lodge. Because most of the Proceedings were found outside of Louisiana, they were the English editions. It should also be noted that as of this time, we know of no copies of the 1813, 14, 15, 16, 17, 19 or 1829 Proceedings of the Grand Lodge of Louisiana. I believe it very possible that mixed in with some lodge records or in a lodge bookcase, drawer, or box of other "stuff" any one of these missing Proceedings can turn up.

Finally, you will notice that some of the terms and practices of the Grand Lodge from the early days differ from today. For example, in the 1818 Proceedings, as well as in a number of the early Proceedings, you will note that the Grand Master is addressed as "Right Worshipful" Grand Master and not "Most Worshipful" as today. Likewise, the Grand Lodge is the "Right Worshipful" Grand Lodge rather than "Most Worshipful" Grand Lodge. Since four of the five lodges that created the Grand Lodge held charters from the Grand Lodge of Pennsylvania (which uses "Right Worshipful" even to this day), I feel it safe in assuming that this is the source for this early practice. Another difference is that today when one is elected Grand Junior Warden, the normal chain of events is to progress yearly up to the office of Grand Master, serve one year in that office and then become a Past Grand Master. In the early days, there seems to have been no formal progressive line other than that one must have served as a Grand Warden before serving as Grand Master (1812 excepted). When someone was elected Grand Master, they could serve a number of years in that office. I believe that this early practice was with the mind that who best can serve the Grand Lodge, will serve, rather than everyone having a chance to serve.

Yes, if we were able to pull someone from the early 1800's and let them visit any lodge of today, we would certainly hear them say, "We didn't do it *that* way in my day!"

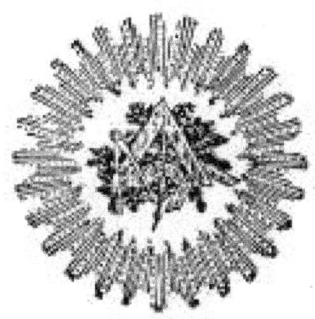

GRAND LODGE

OF THE

Most Ancient and Honorable Fraternity

OF

Free and Accepted Masons

OF THE

STATE OF LOUISIANA.

At a quarterly Communication held in the City of New-Orleans, on Saturday the 26th. day of December, Anno Lucis 5818, in ample forme, were present,

THE BRETHREN :

Lewis Moreau-Lislet, *Grand-Master,*
J. B. Modeste Lefebvre, *Deputy Grand-Master,*
J. B. Desbois, R∴ W∴ *Senior Grand Warden,*
Yves Le Monier, R∴ W∴ *Junior Grand Warden,*
Augustus Guibert, R∴ W∴ *Grand Secretary,*
J. B. Pinta, R∴ W∴ *Grand Treasurer,*

[2]

William S. Hubert, R∴ W∴ *Grand Orator*,
John Pinard, R∴ W∴ *Grand Tyler*,
Stephen Berthel, *Grand Poursuivant*,
Augustin Macarty, *Grand Marshal*;

And all the others Grand Officers, Ex-Grand Officers, and Members of the Grand Lodge and the representatives of the Lodges under the jurisdiction of the Grand Lodge.

The Grand Lodge has been opened according to the usual formes, and it has been proceeded to the election of the Officers for the ensuing year, and the Brethren whose name follow have been duly elected:

THE BRETHREN :

M. Léfebvre, Merchant, R∴ W∴ *Grand-Master*,
J. B. Desbois, Counsellor at Law, R∴ W∴ *Deputy Grand-Master*,
Yves Le Monier, physician, R∴ W∴ *Senior Grand Warden*,
Augustin Macarty, Mayor, R∴ W∴ *Junior Grand Warden*,
N. Visinier, Master of Languages, R∴ W∴ *Grand Secretary*,
John Baptiste Pinta, Gold-Smith, R∴ W∴ *Grand Treasurer*,
D. R. D. Desessart, Secretary of the Mayoralty R∴ W∴ *Grand Orator*,
John Pinard, Merchant, R∴ W∴ *Grand Tyler*,
Stephen Berthel, Merchant, R∴ W∴ *Grand Poursuivant*,
G. Debuys, Merchant, R∴ W∴ *Grand Marshal*.

[3]

The Lodge has then been shut until the General Grand Communication on the 10th. day of the 11th. Month of Masonry 5818.

At a Grand General Communication held in ample forme in the City of New-Orleans, on the 10th. day of the 11th. Month of Masonry of the year 5818, the R∴ W∴ Grand Officers elect, were severally installed according to the ancient usages into their respective offices, and being duly proclaimed they received the cordial and accustomed salutations of the brethren present.

The R∴ W∴ Grand Master, and the R∴ W∴ Senior Grand Warden, appointed immediately after, the Brethren Henry Mathieu and Peter Lartigue Mongrue, Senior and Junior Grand Deacons;

And the Brother R∴ W∴ Grand Secretary has appointed the Brother Peter Morel de Guiramand, Deputy Grand Secretary.

It as been afterwards proceeded to the formation of the committees of the said Grand Lodge and the following brethren have been nominated, to wit :

Committee of Charity.	Committee of Account.
The B∴ Moreau Lislet,	The B∴ Macarty,
Macarty,	J. B. Desbois,
Le Monier,	Le Monier.
Le Noir.	

Committee of Correspon.	Committee of Information.
Moreau Lislet,	Debuys,
J. B. Desbois,	Chatry,
D. R. D. Desessart.	Pinard.

[4]

Committee of Stewardship.

Congourdan,
Auguste Douce,
Chatry.

The Grand Lodge has then been shut in good harmony.

ACTIVE MEMBERS OF THE GRAND LODGE.

L. Moreau Lislet, *Counsellor at Law, Founder, Ex-Grand-Master*,
J. Soulié, *Past Grand-Master, Merchant, Founder*,
F. Dubourg, *Past Grand-Master Mercht. Founder*,
J. B. Labatut, *Merchant, Founder*,
Paul Lanusse, *Merchant, Founder*,
Thomas Urquhart, *Merchant, Founder*,
Joseph Tricou, *Merchant, Founder*,
P. Hardy, *Teacher, Founder*,
Charles Roche, *Book-Seller, Founder*,
Victor-Amédée Bonjean, *Goldsmith, Founder*,
Peter Delino, *Planter, Founder*,
Joseph Eyssalem, *Merchant, Founder*,

A. Guibert, *Cashier of the B. Bank of the State*,
William S. Hubert, *Merchant*,
Auguste Douce, *Cabinet-Maker*,
Spire Loquet, *Master of Languages*,
John Guadiz, *Dentiste*,
Caliste Congourdan, *Undertaker*,
Andrews Clavié, *Merchant*,

[5]

Joseph Le Noir, *Hatter,*
J. B. Gilly, *Merchant,*
L. M. Renaud, *Merchant,*
G. W. Morgan, *Shérif,*
N. Mioton, *Confectioner,*
J. L. F. Chatry, *Clerck to a Notary,*
B. Bacas, *Cabinet-Maker,*
James Rouly, *Artist.*

Representatives of the Lodges of the Jurisdiction.

Gaspard Debuis W∴ Master, L. M. Reynaud S∴ Warden, J. B. Plauché J∴ Warden,	*La Parfaite Union,* No. 1.
No. No. Not represented, No.	*La Charité,* No. 2.
Auguste Douce W∴ Master, Manuel Fleytas S∴ Warden, H. Doiron J∴ Warden,	*La Concorde,* No. 3.
J. Le Noir W∴ Master, J. L. F. Chatry S∴ Warden, F. Dissart J∴ Warden,	*La Persévérance,* No. 4.
J. B. Gilly W∴ Master, B. Bacas S∴ Warden, B. Grima J∴ Warden,	*l'Etoile Polaire,* No. 5.
No. No. Not represented, No.	*La Loge Friendship,* No. 6.
J. Pinard, Representative of the three Lodges *at the Stranger*	*l'Union Fraternelle de la Charité,* No. 7, *Les Amis Réunis,* No. 8, *La Réunion à la Vertu,* No. 9.

[6]

J. P. Morel de Guiramand, Representative	}	*l'Etoile Flamboyante,* No. 10.
J. Pinard, Representative	} *at Sens*	*Le Temple de la Divine Pastorale,* No. 11.
J. P. Morel de Guiramand, Representative	}	*La Vérité,* No. 12.
Gaspard Debuys, Representative	}	*l'Union,* No. 13.
J. Pinard, Representative	} *at Sens*	*La Rectitude,* No. 14.

Expulsions.

Anthony Herès, *No.* 3. *New-Orleans.*
Lewis Romano, *No.* 3. *New-Orleans.*
James Chauvin, *No.* 4. *New-Orleans.*

Attest

Address—to the Grand Lodge of the State of Louisiana

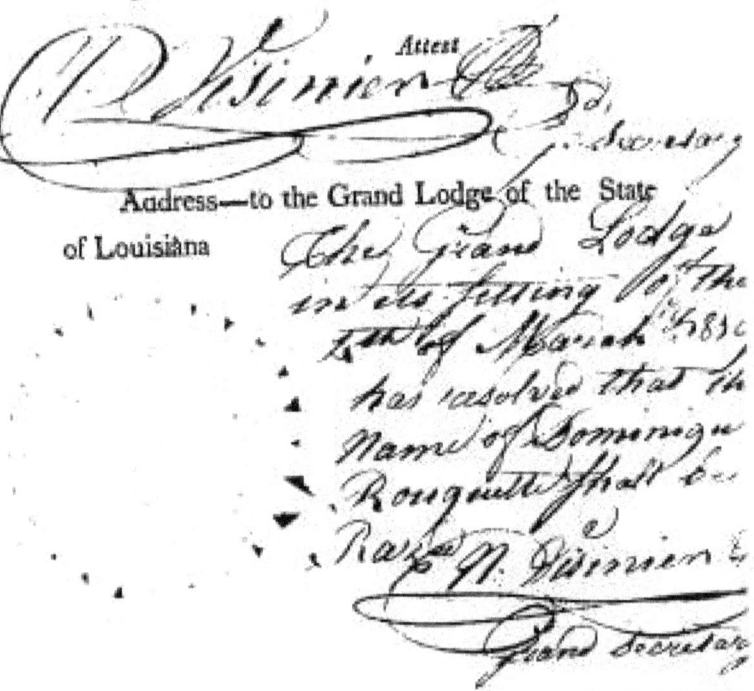

EXTRACT

OF THE

PROCEEDINGS OF THE GRAND LODGE

OF THE

Most Ancient Fraternity

of Free & Accepted Masons

OF THE

STATE OF LOUISIANA

Held in the City of New-Orleans.

Published by order of the Society.

NEW ORLEANS,

PRINTED BY L. FOURCAND.

A∴ L∴ 5820.—A∴ D∴ 1820.

GRAND LODGE

OF THE

Most Ancient & honourable Fraternity
Of free & accepted Masons
OF LOUISIANA.

THE Grand Lodge of Louisiana having met at the hall of their sittings, in the City of New-Orleans, on the twenty-first of December A∴ L∴ 5819, the day of their Grand quarterly Communication & the same having been opened in ample form, the election of the Grand Officers for the ensuing year was proceeded to & the brethren whose names follow were declared to be duly elected, viz :

The M∴ W∴ B∴ Yves Lemonnier,	R∴ W∴ Grand Master,
R∴ W∴ B∴ Augustin Macarty,	*Deputy Grand Master,*
R∴ W∴ B∴ Jn. Francis Canonge,	*Senior Grand Warden,*
R∴ W∴ B∴ Gaspard Debuys,	*Junior Grand Warden,*
W∴ B∴ Francis Dissard,	*Grand Secretary,*
W∴ B∴ John Baptist Pinta,	*Grand Treasurer,*
W∴ B∴ Lewis Moreau Lislet,	G∴ *Chaplain or Orator,*
W∴ B∴ Stephen Bertel, W∴ B∴ John Guadiz,	*Grand Stewarts,*
W∴ B∴ Jn. L. Francis Chatry,	*Grand Sword-bearer or Master of Ceremonies,*
W∴ B∴ Auguste Douce,	*Grand Marshal,*
W∴ B∴ Nicholas Mioton,	*Grand Pursuivant.*

(4)

And on the tenth of January A∴ D∴ 1820, the day of the grand annual & general communication, the several Grand Officers elect were successively installed into their respective offices agreeably to ancient usages, and after being duly proclaimed, they received the cordial & accustomed salutations of all the members present.

The R∴ W∴ Grand Master was pleased to make the following appointements, viz:

Brother P. Lartigue Mongrué, *Senior grand Deacon,*
Brother Anathole Peychaux, *Junior grand Deacon,*
Brother A. Francis Renault, *grand Tyler.*

The R∴ W∴ Grand Master did also appoint the following standing Committees.

Committee of Correspondence.

The R∴ W∴ Brother Lewis Moreau Lislet,
R∴ W∴ Brother Augustin Macarty,
R∴ W∴ Brother John Francis Canonge.

Committee of Accounts.

The R∴ W∴ Brother Modeste Lefebvre,
R∴ W∴ Brother Gaspard Debuys,
R∴ W∴ Brother John Pinard.

Committee of Economy.

The R∴ W∴ Brother John Baptist Pinta,
R∴ W∴ Brother Augustin Macarty,
R∴ W∴ Brother Stephen Bertel.

(5)

LIST

Of the Members of the Grand Lodge of the Louisiana.

GRAND OFFICERS.

The M∴ W∴ Brother Yves Lemonnier, Medecine Doctor, R∴ A∴, K∴ T∴, *Grand Master,*

The R∴ W∴ Brother Augustin Macarty, Mayor of the City of New-Orleans, R∴ A∴, K∴ T∴, *Deputy Grand Master,*

The R∴ W∴ Brother J. Francis Canonge, Counsellor at law, Clerk of the house of Representatives of the State of Louisiana, R∴ A∴, *Senior Grand Warden,*

The R∴ W∴ Brother Gaspard Debuys, Merchant, Master of the W∴ Lodge No. 1, R∴ A∴, *Junior Grand Warden,*

The W∴ Brother Francis Dissard, formerly an Inhabitant of St. Domingo, R∴ A∴ K∴ T∴, *Grand Secretary,*

The W∴ Brother John Baptist Pinta, Jeweller, R∴ A∴, K∴ T∴, *Grand Treasurer,*

The W∴ Brother Lewis Moreau Lislet, Counsellor at law, member of the general Assembly of the State of Louisiana, Past Grand Master, Master of the W∴ Lodge No. 5, R∴ A∴, K∴ T∴, *Grand Chaplain or Orator,*

The W∴ Brother Peter Lartigue Mongrué, Officer in the Navy, R∴ A∴, *Senior Grand Deacon,*

The W∴ Brother Anathole Peychaux, Justice of the Peace in the City of New Orleans, R∴ A∴, *Junior Grand Deacon,*

(6)

The W∴ Brother Stephen Bertel, Architect, R∴ A∴, K∴ T∴,
The W∴ Brother John Guadiz, Dentist, R∴ A∴, K∴ T∴,
} *Grand Stewarts,*

The W∴ Brother John Lewis Francis Chatry, formerly an inhabitant of St. Domingo, Master of the W∴ Lodge No. 4, R∴ A∴ *Grand Sword bearer or Master of Ceremonies,*

The W∴ Brother Augustus Douce, Ebonist, Master of the W∴ Lodge No. 3, R∴ A∴, K∴ T∴, *Grand Marshal,*

The W∴ Brother Nicholas Mioton, Confectionner, R∴ A∴, *Grand Pursuivant.*

Brother Anthony Francis Renault, Painter, M∴ M∴ *Grand Tyler.*

MEMBERS OF THE GRAND LODGE HOLDING NO OFFICE IN THE SAME.

The R∴ W∴ Brother Modeste Lefebvre, Merchant, Past-Grand-Master, R∴ A∴, K∴ T∴.

The R∴ W∴ Brother John Soulié, Merchant, Past-Grand-Master, R∴ A∴.

The R∴ W∴ Brother Peter Francis Dubourg, Merchant, Past-Grand-Master, R∴ A∴.

The R∴ W∴ Brother John Baptist Labatut, Merchant, R∴ A∴.

The R∴ W∴ Brother Paul Lanusse, Merchant, R∴ A∴.

The R∴ W∴ Brother John Pinard, Merchant, R∴ A∴, K∴ T∴.

The R∴ W∴ Brother Thomas Urquhart, Merchant, President of the Louisiana Bank, R∴ A∴.

(7)

The R∴ W∴ Brother Jh. Tricou senior, Merchant.

The R∴ W∴ Brother Peter Hardy, Professor of Languages, R∴ A∴.

The R∴ W∴ Brother Victor Amédée Bonjean, Jeweller, R∴ A∴.

The R∴ W∴ Brother Augustus Guibert, Cashier of the Branch Bank of the State of Louisiana at St. Francisville, R∴ A∴.

The R∴ W∴ Brother Spire Loquet, Professor of Languages, R∴ A∴.

The R∴ W∴ Brother André Clavié, Merchant, R∴ A∴.

The R∴ W∴ Brother John Baptist Gilly, Merchant, R∴ A∴, K∴ T∴.

The R∴ W∴ Brother Lewis Melchior Reynaud, Merchant, R∴ A∴.

The R∴ W∴ Brother George W. Morgan, Sheriff of the Parish of Orleans, R∴ A∴.

The R∴ W∴ Brother Milten-Berger, Medecine Doctor, R∴ A∴.

The R∴ W∴ Brother Bartholomew Bacas, Ebonist, P∴ M∴.

The R∴ W∴ Brother James Rouly, Artist, R∴ A∴.

The R∴ W∴ Brother Morel de Guiramand, Conveyancer, R∴ A∴.

The R∴ W∴ Brother Lewis Fortin, Medecine Doctor, P∴ M∴.

The R∴ W∴ Brother Hyacinthe Hazeur, Gentleman, P∴ M∴.

The R∴ W∴ Brother Hyppolite Doiron, Ebonist, R∴ A∴.

The R∴ W∴ Brother Manuel Fleytas, Gentleman, R∴ A∴, K∴ T∴.

(8)

Officers Representing the several Lodges under the Jurisdiction of the Grand Lodge.

Lodge No. 1,
- Gaspard Debuys, *Master,*
- Amédée Longer, Merchant, R∴ A∴, K∴ T∴, *Senior Warden,*
- Philip Pedesclaux, Notary public, R∴ A∴, K∴ T∴, *Junior Warden.*

Lodge No. 2,
- Peter Derbigny, Judge of the Supreme Court, P∴ M∴, *Master,*
- L. Fortin, P∴ M∴, *Sen∴ Warden,*
- James Pitot, Judge of the Parish of Orleans, M∴, *Junior Warden.*

Lodge No. 3,
- Augustus Douce, *Master,*
- Anathole Peychaux, *Senior Warden,*
- Milten-Berger, *Junior Warden.*

Lodge No. 4,
- J. L. F. Chatry, *Master,*
- Gabriel-Henry Léaumont, an Officer in the Branch Bank of the United States located in the City of New-Orleans, R∴ A∴, *Senior Warden,*
- Anthony Nicholas Lesconflair, Architect, R∴ A∴, *Junior Warden.*

Lodge No. 5,
- L. Moreau Lislet, *Master,*
- Stephen Bertel, *Senior Warden,*
- John Baptist Faget, Merchant, R∴ A∴, K∴ T∴, *Junior Warden.*

Lodge No. 6, Represented by Brother A. Longer, their Proxy.

Lodges No. 7, 8 & 9, Represented by Brother John Pinard, their Proxy.

Logde No. 10, Represented by Brother J. B. Pinta, their Proxy.

Lodge No. 11, No Proxy.

(9)

Lodge No. 12, Represented by Brother L. M. Reynaud, their Proxy.

Lodge No. 13, Represented by Brother Gaspard Debuys, their Proxy.

Lodges No. 14, 15 & 16, } No Proxy.

Lodge No. 17, Represented by Brother John Francis Canonge, their Proxy.

List of Lodges under the Jurisdiction of the Grand Lodge.

La *Parfaite Union*, No. 1, sitting in the City of New-Orleans.

La *Charité*, No. 2, ditto.
La *Concorde*, No. 3, ditto.
La *Persévérance*, No. 4, ditto.
L'*Etoile Polaire*, No. 5, ditto.

Friendship, No. 6, at Mobile, Alabama Territory.

La *Union Fraternal de Caridad*, No. 7, ⎫
Los *Amigos Reunidos*, No. 8, ⎬ In the Spanish dominions.
La *Réunion à la Virtud*, No. 9, ⎭

L'*Etoile Flamboyante*, No. 10, at Bâton-Rouge, State of Louisiana.

El Templo de la Divina Pastora, No. 11, in the Spanish possessions.

La *Vérité*, No. 12, at Donaldsonville, (Louisiana.)

L'*Union*, No. 13, at Natchitoches, (Louisiana.)

Rectitude, No. 14, sitting in the Spanish dominions.

Columbian, No. 15, at Alexandrie, (Louisiana.)

Eureka, No. 16, at Blakeley, Alabama Territory.

Wasihngton, No. 17, at Bâton-Rouge, (Louisiana.)

(10)

EXPULSIONS.

Joseph Flee, Lodge No. 3, for conduct unworthy of a Mason.

Joseph Dorfeuille, Lodge No. 5, for non payment of dues.

Most Wor∴ Brother,

Agreeably to the regulations of the Grand Lodge, I have the honour to forward to you one copy of the List of the Grand Officers for the masonic year 5820 & members of the same, together with the list of the expulsions which were communicated to that body during the last year.

With sentiments of high regard, I am

Most W∴ Brother

Your devoted & affectionate Brother,

Dissard

N a. The Grand Secretary's Adress, is FRANCIS DISSARD, Esquire,—New-Orleans.

EXTRACT
OF THE
PROCEEDINGS
OF THE
GRAND LODGE
OF THE
Most Ancient Fraternity
OF
FREE & ACCEPTED MASONS
OF THE
STATE OF LOUISIANA,
Held in the City of New-Orleans.

Published by order of the Society.

NEW-ORLEANS,
PRINTED BY L. FOURCAND.

A∴ L∴ 5821.—A∴ D∴ 1821.

GRAND LODGE

OF THE

Most Ancient & Honourable Fraternity of Free & Accepted Masons of Louisiana.

THE Grand Lodge of Louisiana having met a the hall of their sittings, in the City of New-Orleans, the 30th. day of the 10th. month A∴ L∴ 5820, the day of their grand quartely communication & the same having been opened in ample form, the election of the Grand Officers for the ensuing year was proceeded to & the brethren whose names follow were declared to be duly elected, VIZ:

The M∴ W∴ B∴ Augustin Macarty,	R∴ W∴ *Grand Master,*
R∴ W∴ B∴ John Francis Canonge,	*Deputy Grand Master,*
R∴ W∴ B∴ Gaspard Debuys,	*Senior Grand Warden,*
R∴ W∴ B∴ Anathole Peychaud,	*Junior Grand Warden,*
W∴ B∴ Francis Dissard,	*Grand Secretary,*
W∴ B∴ George W∴ Morgan,	*Grand Treasurer,*
W∴ B∴ Lewis Moreau Lislet,	G∴ *Chaplain or Orator,*
W∴ B∴ John Guadiz, W∴ B∴ Stephen Bertel,	*Grand Stewarts,*
W∴ B∴ John Baptist Faget,	*Grand Sword-bearer or Master of Ceremonies,*
W∴ B∴ Nicholas Lesconflair,	*Grand Marshal,*
W∴ B∴ Nicholas Mioton,	*Grand Pursuivant.*

(4)

And the 14th. day of January A∴ D∴ 1821, the day of the grant annual & general communication, the several Grand Officers elect were successively installed into their respective offices agreably to ancient usages, and after being duly proclaimed, they received the cordial & accustomed salutations of all the members present.

The R∴ W∴ Grand Master was pleased to make the following appointements, viz:

Brother P. Lartigue Mongrué, *Senior Grand Deacon*,
Bartholomew Bacas, *Junior Grand Deacon*.

Committee of Correspondence.

The R∴ W∴ Brother *John Francis* Canonge,
R∴ W∴ Brother *Gaspard* Debuys,
R∴ W∴ Brother *Lewis* Moreau Lislet.

Committee of Accounts.

The R∴ W∴ Brother *Yves* Lemonnier,
R∴ W∴ Brother Milten Berger,
R∴ W∴ Brother *Nicholas* Lesconflair.

Committee of Information.

The R∴ W∴ Brother *Anathole* Peychaud,
R∴ W∴ Brother *Modeste* Lefebvre.
R∴ W∴ Brother *Lewis Melchior* Reynaud.

Committee of Economy.

The R∴ W∴ Brother *Peter* Lartigue Mongrué,
R∴ W∴ Brother *Gabriel Henry* Léaumont,
R∴ W∴ Brother *Bartholomew* Bacas.

(5)

LIST

Of the Members of the Grand Lodge of the Louisiana.

GRAND OFFICERS.

The M∴ W∴ Brother Augustin Macarty, R∴ A∴, K∴ T∴, *Grand Master,*

The R∴ W∴ Brother J. Francis Canonge, Counsellor at law, R∴ A∴, K∴ T∴, *Deputy Gd∴ Master,*

The R∴ W∴ Brother Gaspard Debuys, Merchant, R∴ A∴, *Senior Grand Warden,*

The R∴ W∴ Anathole Peychaud, Justice of the Peace, in the City of New-Orleans, R∴ A∴, K∴ T∴, *Junior Grand Warden,*

The R∴ W∴ Brother Yves Lemonnier, Medecine Doctor, R∴ A∴, K∴ T∴, *Past-Grand-Master,*

The W∴ Brother Francis Dissard, formerly an Inhabitant of St. Domingo, R∴ A∴, K∴ T∴, *Grand Secretary,*

The W∴ Brother George W. Morgan, Sheriff of the Parish of Orleans, P∴ M∴, *Grand Treasurer,*

The W∴ Brother Lewis Moreau Lislet, Counsellor at law, Past-Grand-Master, R∴ A∴, K∴ T∴, *Grand Chaplain or Orator,*

The W∴ Brother Peter Lartigue Mongrué, Officer in the Navy, R∴ A∴, *Senior Grand Deacon,*

The W∴ Brother Batholomew Bacas, Ebonist, P∴ M∴ *Junior Grand Deacon,*

(6)

The W∴ Brother John Guadiz, Dentist, R∴ A∴, K∴ T∴,
The W∴ Brother Stephen Bertel, Architect, R∴ A∴, K∴ T∴,
} *Grand Stewarts,*

The W∴ Brother John Baptist Faget, Merchant, R∴ A∴ K∴ T∴,   *Grand Sword bearer or Master of Ceremonies,*

The W∴ Brother Nicholas Lesconflair, Architect, R∴ A∴, K∴ T∴,   *Grand Marshal,*

The W∴ Brother Nicholas Mioton, Confectionner, R∴ A∴,   *Grand Pursuivant,*

Brother Anthony Francis Renault, Painter, M∴,   *Grand Tyler.*

Members of the Grand Lodge Holding no Office in the same.

The R∴ W∴ Brother Modeste Lefebvre, Merchant, Past-Grand-Master, R∴ A∴, K∴ T∴

The R∴ W∴ Brother John Soulié, Past-Grand-Master, R∴ A∴

The R∴ W∴ Brother Peter Francis Dubourg, Merchant, Past-Grand-Master, R∴ A∴

The R∴ W∴ Brother John Baptist Labatut, Merchant, R∴ A∴

The R∴ W∴ Brother Paul Lanusse, Merchant, R∴ A∴

The R∴ W∴ Brother Thomas Hurquhart, Mercht. R∴ A∴

(7)

The R∴ W∴ Brother Peter Hardy, Professor of languages, R∴ A∴

The R∴ W∴ Brother Joseph Tricou senior, Merchant, R∴ A∴

The R∴ W∴ Brother Victor Amédée Bonjean, Jeweller, R∴ A∴

The R∴ W∴ Brother Spire Loquet, Professor of languages, R∴ A∴

The R∴ W∴ Brother Andrew Clavié, Merchant, R∴ A∴

The R∴ W∴ Brother John Baptist Gilly, Merchant, R∴ A∴, K∴ T∴

The R∴ W∴ Brother Lewis Melchior Reynaud, Merchant, R∴ A∴

The R∴ W∴ Brother James Rouly, Artist, R∴ A∴

The R∴ W∴ Brother Morel de Guiramand, Conveyancer, R∴ A∴

The R∴ W∴ Brother Augustus Douce, Ebonist, R∴ A∴, K∴ T∴

The R∴ W∴ Brother Milten Berger, Medecine Doctor, R∴ A∴

The R∴ W∴ Brother Lewis Fortin, Medecine Doctor, P∴ M∴

The R∴ W∴ Brother Hyppolite Doiron, Ebonist, R∴ A∴

The R∴ W∴ Brother Manuel Fleytas, Gentleman, R∴ A∴, K∴ T∴

(8)

Officers Representing the several Lodges under the Jurisdiction of the Grand Lodge.

Lodge No. 1, { Lewis Melchior Reynaud, *Master,*
George W. Morgan, *Senior Warden,*
Jn. Baptist Plauché, Merchant, R∴ A∴, *Junior Warden.*

Lodge No. 2, { John Francis Canonge, *Master,*
Yves Lemonnier, *Senior Warden,*
Peter Lewis Morel, Counsellor at law, *Junior Warden.*

Lodge No. 3, { Anathole Peychaud, *Master,*
Milten Berger, *Senior Warden,*
Henry Bebee, Painter, P∴ M∴, *Junior Warden.*

Lodge No. 4, { J. J. Chessé, Gentleman, R∴ A∴, *Master,*
Gabriel Henry Léaumont, R∴ A∴, *Senior Warden,*
Peter Lartigue Mongrué, *Junior Warden.*

Lodge No. 5, { Lewis Moreau Lislet, *Master,*
John Baptist Faget, *Senior Warden,*
Lewis J. Dufilho, Apohticary, R∴ A∴, K∴ T∴, *Junior Warden.*

Lodge No. 6, { By a Resolution of the W∴ Grand Lodge, under date of the 1st. July 1820, her Charter was withdrawn.

Lodges No. 7, 8 & 9, { No Proxy.

Lodge No. 10, { Represented by Brother Francis Dissard, their Proxy.

Lodge No. 11, No Proxy.

Lodge No. 12, { Represented by Brother Lewis Melchior Reynaud, their Proxy.

Lodge No. 13, { Represented by Brother Gaspard Debuys, their Proxy.

(9)

Lodges No. 14, 15 & 16, } No Proxy.

Lodge No. 17, { Represented by Brother John Francis Canouge, their Proxy.

Loge No. 18, No Proxy.

Lodge No. 19, { Represented by Brother Philip Pédesclaux, their Proxy.

Lodge No. 20, { Lewis Duhart, Professor of languages, P∴ M∴, *Master*,
Jh. Caliste Cougourdan, Architect, R∴ A∴, *Senior Warden*,
Anthony Lamy Soulmon, School Master, *Junior Warden*.

List of Lodges under the Jurisdiction of the Grand Lodge.

La *Parfaite-Union*, No. 1, sitting in the city of New-Orleans.
La *Charité*, No. 2, ditto.
La *Concorde*, No. 3, ditto.
La *Persévérance*, No. 4, ditto.
L'*Etoile-Polaire*, No. 5, ditto.
La *Union Fraternal de Caridad*, No. 7, ⎫
Los *Amigos Reunidos*, No. 8, ⎬ In the Spanish Dominions.
La *Réunion à la Virtud*, No. 9, ⎭
L'*Etoile Flamboyante*, No. 10, at Bâton-Rouge, (Louisiana.)
El *Templo de la Divina Pastora*, No. 11, in the Spanish domis.
La *Vérité*, No. 12, at Donalsonville, (Louisiana.)
L'*Union*, No. 13, at Natchitoches, (Louisiana.)
Rectitude, No. 14, sitting in the Spanish dominions.
Columbian, No. 15, at Alexandria, (Louisiana.)
Eureka, No. 16, at Blakeley, Alabama Territory.
Washington, No. 17, at Bâton-Rouge, (Louisiana.)
La *Aurora de Yucatan*, No. 18, in the Spanish dominions.
L'*Humble Chaumière*, No. 19, at St. Landry, County of Oppeloussas.
La *Triple Bienfaisance*, No. 20, at New-Orleans.

(10)

EXPULSIONS.

Félix Durousseau, of Lodge No. 3, for malversation Treasurer of said Lodge.

John Lewis Francis Chatry, of Lodge No. 4, for non payment of his dues.

Joakim de la Vega, for having proved to be of bad temper

Miguel Sanchez & Nicanor de Obares, of Lodge No. 11, f having spoken injuriously of, and depreciated Masonr and not paying their dues.

Most Wor∴ Brother,

Agreeably to the regulations of the Grand Lodge, I ha the honour to forward to you one copy of the list of the Gra Officers for the masonic year 5821 & members of the sar together with the list of the expulsions which were commu cated to that body during the last year.

With sentiments of high regard, I am
Most W∴ Brother
Your devoted & affectionate Broth

[signature]

N.a. The Grand Secretary's Adress, is FRAN∙ DISSARD, Esquire,—New-Orleans.

EXTRACT
OF THE
PROCEEDINGS
OF THE
GRAND LODGE
OF THE
Most Ancient Fraternity
OF
FREE & ACCEPTED MASONS
OF THE
STATE OF LOUISIANA,
Held in the City of New-Orleans.

Published by order of the Society.

NEW-ORLEANS,
PRINTED BY B∴ L. FOURCAND.

A∴ L∴ 5821.—A∴ D∴ 1822.

GRAND LODGE

OF THE

Most Ancient & Honourable Fraternity of Free & Accepted Masons of Louisiana.

THE Grand Lodge of Louisiana having met a the hall of their sittings, in the City of New-Orleans, the 29th. day of the 10th. month A∴ L∴ 5821, the day of their Grand quartely Communication & the same having been opened in ample form, the election of the Grand Officers for the ensuing year was proceeded to & the brethren whose names follow were declared to be duly elected, VIZ:

The M. W. B. *J. Francis* CANONGE, R∴ W∴ *Grand Master*,
 R. W. B. *Gaspard* DEBUYS, *Deputy Grand Master*,
 R. W. B. *Yves* LEMONNIER, *Senior Grand Warden*,
 R. W. B. *G. H. de* LEAUMONT, *Junior Grand Warden*,
  W. B. *Francis* DISSARD, *Grand Secretary*,
  W. B. *George W.* MORGAN, *Grand Treasurer*,
  W. B. *L.* MOREAU LISLET, *Gd∴ Chaplain or Orator*,
  W. B. MILTENBERGER, } *Grand Stewarts*,
  W. B. *J. H.* HOLLAND,   }
  W. B. *Lewis* DUHART, *Grand Sword-Bearer or Master of Ceremonies*,
  W. B. *Augustus* DOUCE, *Grand Marshal*,
  W. B. *Amédée* LONGER, *Grand Pursuivant*.

(4)

And the 13th. day of January A∴ D∴ 1822, the day of the grant annual & general communication, the several Grand Officers elect were successively installed into their respective offices agreably to ancient usages, and after being duly proclaimed, they received the cordial & accustomed salutations of all the members present.

The R∴ W∴ Grand Master was pleased to make the following appointements, VIZ:

Brother *John Baptist* Faget, *Senior Grand Deacon*,
Philip Pédesclaux, *Junior Grand Deacon.*

Committee of Correspondence.

The R. W. B. *Lewis* Moreau Lislet,
R. W. B. *George W.* Morgan,
R. W. B. *Anatole* Peychaud.

Committee of Accounts.

The R. W. B. *Gaspard* Debuys,
R. W. B. *John Baptist* Faget,
R. W. B. Miltenberger.

Committee of Information.

The R. W. B. *Lewis Melchior* Raynaud,
R. W. B. *John* Guadiz,
R. W. B. *Frederic* Letanneur.

Committee of Economy.

The R. W. B. *Amédée* Longer,
R. W. B. *Bartholomew* Bacas,
R. W. B. *Stephen* Bertel.

(5)

LIST *of the Members of the Grand Lodge of the Louisiana.*

GRAND OFFICERS.

The M. W. B. *John Francis* Canonge, Consellor at law, R∴ A∴, K∴ T∴.   *Grand Master.*

The R. W. B. *Gaspard* Debuys, Merchant, R∴ A∴.   *Deputy Grand Master.*

The R. W. B. *Yves* Lemonnier, Medecine Doctor, R∴ A∴, K∴ T∴.   *Senior Grand Warden.*

The R. W. B. *Gabriel Henry* De Léaumont, an Officer the Bank, R∴ A∴ *Junior Grand Warden.*

The R. W. B. *Augustin* Macarty, R∴ A∴, K∴ T∴.   *Past-Grand-Master.*

The W. B. *Francis* Dissard, formerly an Inabitant of St. Domingo, R∴ A∴, K∴ T∴ *Grand Secretary.*

The W. B. *George W.* Morgan, Sheriff of the Parish of Orleans, R∴ A∴.   *Grand Treasurer.*

The W. B. *Lewis* Moreau Lislet, Counsellor at law, Past-Grand-Master, R∴ A∴, K∴ T∴. *Grand Chaplain or Orateur.*

The W. B. *John Baptist* Faget, Merchant, R∴ A∴, K∴ T∴.   *Senior Grand Deacon.*

The W. B. *Philip* Pédesclaux, Notary, R∴ A∴, K∴ T∴.   *Junior Grand Deacon.*

The W. B. Miltenberger, Medecine Doctor, R∴ A∴.
The W. B. *J. H.* Holland, Deputy Sheriff, R∴ A∴, K∴ T∴. } *Grand Stewarts.*

(6)

The W. B. *Lewis* Duhart, Professor of Languages, P∴ M∴   Grand Sword-Bearer or Master of Ceremony.

The W. B. *Augustus* Douce, Ebonist, R∴ A∴, K∴ T∴   Grand Marshal.

The W. B. *Amédée* Longer, Merchant, R∴ A∴, K∴ T∴   Grand Pursuivant.

Brother *Anthony Francis* Renault, Painter. M∴   Grand Tyler.

Members of the Grand Lodge Holding no Office in the same.

The R. W. B. *Modeste* Lefebvre, Merchant, Past-Grand-Master, R∴ A∴, K∴ T∴.

The R. W. B. *Peter Francis* Dubourg, Merchant, Past-Grand-Master, R∴ A∴.

The R. W. B. *John* Soulié, Merchant, Past-Grand-Master, R∴ A∴.

The R. W. B. *John Baptist* Labatut, Merchant, R∴ A∴.

The R. W. B. *Paul* Lanusse, Merchant, R∴ A∴.

The R. W. B. *Thomas* Hurquhart, Merchant, R∴ A∴.

The R. W. B. *Peter* Hardy, Professor of languages, R∴ A∴.

The R. W. B. *Joseph* Tricou senior, R∴ A∴.

The R. W. B. *Victor Amédée* Bonjean, Jeweller, R∴ A∴.

(7)

The R. W. B. *Peter* Lartigue Mongrué, Officer in the Navy, R∴ A∴

The R. W. B. *Stephen* Bertel, Architect, R∴ A∴, K∴ T∴

The R. W. B. *Spire* Loquet, Pofessor of languages, R∴ A∴

The R. W. B. *Bartholomew* Bacas, Ebonist, P∴ M∴

The R. W. B. *John* Guadiz, Dentist, R∴ A∴, K∴ T∴

The R. W. B. *Anatole* Peychaud, Justice of the Peace, R∴ A∴, K∴ T∴

The R. W. B. *Nicholas* Lesconflair, Architect, R∴ A∴, K∴ T∴

The R. W. B. *John Baptist* Gilly, Merchant, R∴ A∴, K∴ T∴

The R. W. B. *Nicholas* Mioton, Confectionner, R∴ A∴

The R. W. B. *Lewis Melchior* Reynaud, Merchant, R∴ A∴

The R. W. B. *James* Rouly, R∴ A∴

The R. W. B. Morel de Guiramand, R∴ A∴

The R. W. B. *Lewis* Fortin, Medecine Doctor, P. M∴

The R. W. B. *Hyppolite* Doiron, Ebonist, R∴ A∴

The R. W. B. *Manuel* Fleytas, Gentleman, R∴ A∴, K∴ T∴

The R. W. B. *Jh. Caliste* Cougourdan, Architect, R∴ A∴

(8)

The R. W. B. *Lewis J.* Dufilho, Apothecary, R∴ A∴, K∴ T∴.

The R. W. B. *James* Dulac, Merchant, R∴ A∴.

The R. W. B. *John Baptist* Plauché, Merchant, R∴ A∴.

The R. W. B. *Henry* Bebee, Painter, R∴ A∴.

The R. W. B. *A. M. René* Lamy Soulmon, Pofessor of Languages, P∴ M∴.

The R. W. B. *Bartholomew* Grima, Merchant, P∴ M∴.

The R. W. B. *Francico Xavier* Martinez y Pizarro, R∴ A∴, K∴ T∴.

Officers Representing the several Lodges under the Jurisdiction of the Grand Lodge.

No. 1,
- *G. W.* Morgan, Master,
- *D.* Barthe, Gentleman, R∴ A∴ Senior Warden,
- *H. R.* Denis, Counsellor at law, R∴ A∴ Junior Warden.

No. 2, Represented by N∴ N∴ N∴.

No. 3,
- *Anatole* Peychaud, Master,
- *James* Vienne, Merchant, R∴ A∴ Senior Warden,
- *C L.* Garnier, Merchant, R∴ A∴ Junior Warden.

No. 4,
- *Lewis Alexander Faustin* de Bodin, an Officer in the Bank, R∴ A∴ Master,
- *Nicholas* Morlot, Merchant, M∴ Senior Warden,
- *Charles* Kroll, Sea-man, M∴ Junior Warden.

No. 5,
- *Lewis* Moreau Lislet, Master,
- *Peter* Roche, Printer, M∴ Senior Warden,
- *J. H.* Holland, R∴ A∴, K∴ T∴ Junior Warden.

No. 6, Their Charter has been withdrawn by a resolution of the Grand Lodge.

No. 7, Have returned their Charter.

No. 8, No Proxy.

(9)

No. 9, Represented by Brother John Guadiz, their Proxy.
No. 10, Represented by Brother F. Dissard, their Proxy.
No. 11, Have returned their Charter.
No. 12, Represented by Brot. L. M. Reynaud, their Proxy.
No. 13, Represented by Brother G. Delsuys, their Proxy.
No. 14, 15 & 16, No Proxy.
No. 17, Represented by Brother J. F. Canonge, their proxy.
No. 18, No Proxy.
No. 19, Represented by Brot. Ph. Pédesclaux, their proxy.
No. 20, { Lewis Duhart, *Master*, Fréderic Letanneur, M∴ *Senior Warden*, Bazile Beauregard, M∴ *Junior Warden*.
No. 21, Represented by Brother Y. Lamonnier, their proxy.
No. 22, No Proxy.

List of Lodges under the Jurisdiction of the Grand Lodge.

La *Parfaite-Union*, No. 1, sitting in the city of New-Orleans.
La *Charité*, No. 2, ditto.
La *Concorde*, No. 3, ditto.
La *Persévérance*, No. 4, ditto.
L'*Etoile-Polaire*, No. 5, ditto.
Los *Amigos Reunidos*, No. 8, in the Spanishs Dominions.
La *Réunion à la Virtud*, No. 9, ditto.
L'*Etoile Flamboyante*, No. 10, at Bâton-Rouge, (Louisiana.)
La *Vérité*, No. 12, at Donalsonville, (Louisiana.)
L'*Union*, No. 13, at Natchitoches, (Louisiana.)
Rectitude, No. 14, sitting in the Spanish dominions.
Columbian, No. 15, at Alexandria, (Louisiana.)
Eureka, No. 16, at Blakeley, State of Alabama.
Washington, No. 17, at Bâton-Rouge, (Louisiana.)
La *Aurora de Yucatan*, No. 18, in the Spanish dominions.
L'*Humble Chaumière*, No. 19, at St. Landry, (Louisiana.)
La *Triple Bienfaisance*, No. 20, at New-Orleans.
La *Sincère Vérité*, No. 21, at St. Martin-ville, (Louisiana.)
Mobile Lodge, No. 22, at Mobile, (Alabama.)

(10)

EXPULSIONS.

Félix Durousseau, of Lodge No. 3, for malversatio
Treasurer of said Lodge,—& Joseph Flee, Lodge N
for conduct unworthy of a Mason.

John Lewis Francis Chairy, of Lodge No. 4, for non
ment of his dues.

Joseph Dorfeuil & Manuel Prados, of Lodge No. 5
non payment of his dues.

Reinstated.

Joseph Sanches, of Lodge No. 4.

Most Wor∴ Brother,

*Agreeably to the regulations of the Grand Lodge, I
the honour to forward to you one copy of the list of the G
Officers for the masonic year 5821 & members of the
together with the list of the expulsions which were comm
cated.*

*With sentiments of high regard, I am
Most W∴ Brother,
Your devoted & affectionate Br*

Na. The Grand Secretary's Adress, is Fra
Discard, Esquire,—New-Orleans.

EXTRACT

OF THE

PROCEEDINGS

OF THE

GRAND LODGE

OF THE

Most Ancient Fraternity

OF

FREE & ACCEPTED MASONS

OF THE

STATE OF LOUISIANA,

Held in the City of New-Orleans.

Published by order of the Society.

NEW-ORLEANS,

PRINTED BY L. FOURCAND.

A∴ L∴ 5822.—A∴ D∴ 1823.

GRAND LODGE

OF THE

Most Ancient & Honourable Fraternity of Free & Accepted Masons of Louisiana.

THE Grand Lodge of Louisiana having met a the hall of their sittings, in the City of New-Orleans, the 28th day of the 10th month A∴ L∴ 5822, the day of their Grand quartely Communication & the same having been opened in ample form, the election of the Grand Officers for the ensuing year was proceeded to & the brethren whose names follow were declared to be duly elected, VIZ:

The M. W. B. *Dominick F.* BURTHE, R∴ W∴ Grand Master,
R. W. B. *Gaspard* DEBUYS, Deputy Grand Master,
R. W. B. *Lewis* MOREAU LISLET, Senior Grand Warden,
R. W. B. *L. A. Faustin* DE BODIN, Junior Grand Warden,
W. B. *Francis* DISSARD, Grand Secretary,
W. B. *George W.* MORGAN, Grand Treasurer,
W. B. *Lewis* DUHART, Gd. Chaplain or Orator,
W. B. C. MILTENBERGER,
W. B. *J. H.* HOLLAND, } Grands Stwarts,
W. B. *Augustus* DOUCE, Grand Sword-Bearer or Master of Ceremonies,
W. B. *Fréderic* LETANNEUR, Grand Marshal,
W. B. *Amédée* LONGER, Grand Pursurvant.

(4)

The 12th day of January A∴ D∴ 1823, the day of the grand annual & general communication, the several Grand Officers elected were successively installed into their respective offices, agreeably to ancient usage; and after being duly proclaimed, they received the cordial & accustomed salutations of all the members present.

And on the 8th day of the 12th month A∴ L∴ 5822, at an extra meeting, the new Grand Master appointed the following Grand Officers:

Brother *Lewis J.* DUFILHO, *Senior Grand Deacon,*
　　John Baptist FAGET, *Junior Grand Deacon.*

Committee of Correspondence.

The R. W. B. *John Francis* CANONGE,
R. W. B. *Yves* LEMONNIER,
R. W. B. *Amédée* LONGER.

Committee of Accounts.

The R. W. B. *Lewis* MOREAU LISLET,
R. W. B. *Gaspard* DEBUYS,
R. W. B. *L. A. Faustin* DE BODIN.

Committee of Information.

The R. W. B. *C.* MILTENBERGER,
R. W. B. *Lewis* DUHART,
R. W. B. *Stephen* BERTEL.

Committee of Economy.

The R. W. B. *J. H.* HOLLAND,
R. W. B. *Augustus* DOUCE,
R. W. B. *Gabriel* DE LEAUMONT.

(5)

LIST *of the Members of the Grand Lodge of the Louisiana.*

GRAND OFFICERS.

The M. W. B. Dominick Francis *Burthe*, Gentleman, R∴ A∴,   *Grand Master.*

The R. W. B. Gaspard *Debuys*, Merchant, R∴ A∴,   *Deputy Grand Master.*

The R. W. B. Lewis *Moreau Lislet*, Counsellor at law, Past-Grand Master, R∴ A∴, K∴ T∴, *Senior Grand Warden.*

The R. W. B. Lewis Alexander Faustin *De Bodin*, an Officer the Bank, R∴ A∴, *Junior Gd. Warden.*

The R. W. B. John Francis *Canonge*, Cunsellor at law, R∴ A∴, K∴ T∴,   *Past-Grand Master.*

The W. B. Francis *Dissard*, formerly an Inabitant of St. Domingo, R∴ A∴, K∴ T∴, *Grand Secretary.*

The W. B. George W. *Morgan*, Sheriff of the Parish of Orleans, R∴ A∴,   *Grand Treasurer.*

The W. B. Lewis *Duhart*, Professor of Languages, R∴ A∴,   *Grand Chaplain or Orator.*

The W. B. Lewis J. *Dufilho*, Apothecary, R∴ A∴ K∴ T∴,   *Senior Grand Deacon.*

The W. B. John Baptist *Faget*, Merchant, R∴ A∴ K∴ T∴,   *Junior Grand Deacon.*

The W. B. C. *Miltenberger*, Medecine Doctor, R∴ A∴,

The W. B. J. H. *Holland*, Deputy Sheriff, R∴ A∴, K∴ T∴,   } *Grand Stewarts.*

(6)

The W. B. Augustus *Douce*, Ebonist, R∴ A∴, K∴ T∴ Gd. Sword-bearer or *Master of Ceremony*.

The W. B. Frédéric *Letanneur*, Merchant, R∴ A∴, *Grand Marshal*.

The W. B. Amédée *Longer*, Merchant, R∴ A∴, K∴ T∴, *Grand Pursuivant*.

Brother Francis *Chabran*, R∴ A∴, *Grand Tyler*.

Members of the Grand Lodge Holding no Office in the same.

The R. W. B. Modeste *Lefebvre*, Merchant, Past-Grand-Master, R∴ A∴, K∴ T∴.

The R. W. B. John *Soulié*, Merchant, Past-Grand-Master, R∴ A∴.

The R. W. B. Yves *Lemonnier*, Medecine Doctor, Past-Grand-Master, R∴ A∴, K∴ T∴.

The R. W. B. Augustin *Macarty*, Past-Grand-Master, R∴ A∴, K∴ T∴.

The R. W. B. John Baptist *Labatut*, Merchant, R∴ A∴.

The R. W. B. Victor Amédée *Bonjean*, Jeweller, R∴ A∴.

The R. W. B. Stephen *Bertel*, Architect, R∴ A∴, K∴ T∴.

The R. W. B. Peter *Lartigue Mongrué*, Officer in the Navy, R∴ A∴.

The R. W. B. Spire *Loquet*, Professor of languages, R∴ A∴.

The R. W. B. Bartholomew *Bacas*, Ebon. P∴ M∴.

The R. W. B. John *Guadiz*, Dentist, R∴ A∴, K∴ T∴.

(7)

The R. W. B. Anatole *Peychaud*, Justice of the Peace, R∴ A∴, K∴ T∴

The R. W. B. Nicholas *Lesconflair*, Architect, R∴ A∴, K∴ T∴

The R. W. B. John Baptist *Gilly*, Merchant, R∴ A∴, K∴ T∴

The R. W. B. N. *Mioton*, Confectionner, R∴ A∴

The R. W. B. Lewis M. *Reynaud*, Mercht, R∴ A∴

The R. W. B. Hyppolite *Doiron*, Ebonist, R∴ A∴

The R. W. B. Manuel *Fleytas*, Gentleman, R∴ A∴, C∴ T∴

The R. W. B. Joseph Calixte *Cougourdan*, Architect, R∴ A∴, K∴ T∴

The R. W. B. James *Dulac*, Merchant, R∴ A∴

The R. W. B. John B. Plauché, Merchant, R∴ A∴

The R. W. B. Henry *Bebee*, Painter, R∴ A∴

The R. W. B. Bartholomew *Grima*, Merch. P∴ M∴

The R. W. B. Philip *Pédesclaux*, Notary, R∴ A∴ K∴ T∴

The R. W. B. F. Xavier *Martinez y Pizarro*, R∴ A∴, K∴ T∴

The R. W. B. H. R. *Denis*, Counsellor at law, R∴ A∴

The R. W. B. James *Vienne*, Merchant, R∴ A∴

The R. W. B. C. L. *Garnier*, Merchant, R∴ A∴

The R. W. B. Charles *Kroll*, Officer in the Navy, R∴ A∴

The R. W. B. Peter *Roche*, Printer, P∴ M∴

The R. W. B. Bazile *Beauregard*, Mercht. P∴ M∴

(8)

OFFICERS *Representing the several Lodges under the Jurisdiction of the Grand Lodge.*

No. 1, { D. F. *Burthe*, Master,
Charles *Maurian*, Justice of the Peace, R∴ A∴, K∴ T∴, Junior Warden.
Peter Anthony *Rousseau*, R∴ A∴, Senior Warden,

No. 2, { Its Constitutions have been withdrawn for not having met during one year.

No. 3, { Anatole *Peychaud*, Master,
Charles-L. *Garnier*, Senior Warden,
Félix-F. *Brunet*, R∴ A∴, Junior Warden.

No. 4, { L. A. Faustin *De Bodin*, Master,
Joseph *Sanchez*, Medecine Doctor, R∴ A∴, Senior Warden,
Peter *Chevalier*, Apothecary, R∴ A∴, Junior Warden.

No. 5, { Lewis *Moreau Lislet*, Master,
J. H. *Holland*, Senior Warden,
Lewis Jph. *Even*, Artist, R∴ A∴, Junior Warden.

No. 6, { Their Charter has been withdrawn by a resolution of the Grand Lodge.

No. 7, Have returned their Charter.

No. 8, No Proxy.

No. 9, Represented by Brother John *Guadiz*, their Proxy.

No. 10, Represented by Brother F. *Dissard*, their Proxy.

No. 11, Have returned their Charter.

No. 12, Represented by Brot. L. M. *Reynaud*, their Proxy.

No. 13, Represented by Brother G. *Debuys*, their Proxy.

No. 14, The W. Master has returned its Charter.

No. 15 & 16, No Proxy.

(9)

No. 17, Represented by Brother J. F. Canonge, their Proxy.

No. 18, No Proxy.

No. 19, Represented by Brot. Ph. Pédesclaux, their Proxy.

No. 20,
{ Lewis Duhart,   Master,
René Lemonnier, Medecine Doctor, R∴ A∴,   Senior Warden,
Peter Blanchard, Dentist, P∴ M∴, Junior Warden.

No. 21, Represented by Brother Y. Lemonnier, their Proxy.

No. 22, No Proxy.

LIST *of Lodges under the Jurisdiction of the Grand Lodge.*

La *Parfaite-Union*, No. 1, sitting in the city of New-Orleans.
La *Concorde*,   No. 3, ditto.
La *Persévérance*, No. 4, ditto.
L'*Etoile-Polaire*, No. 5, ditto.
Los *Amigos Reunidos*, No. 8, in the Spanish Dominions.
La *Réunion à la Virtud*, No. 9,   ditto.
L'*Etoile Flamboyante*, No. 10, at Bâton-Rouge, (Louisiana.)
La *Vérité*,   No. 12, at Donalsonville, (Louisiana.)
L'*Union*,   No. 13, at Natchitoches, (Louisiana.)
Columbian,   No. 15, at Alexandria, (Louisiana.)
Eureka,   No. 16, at Blakeley, State of Alabama.
Washington, No. 17, at Bâton-Rouge, (Louisiana.)
La *Aurora de Yucatan*, No. 18, in the Spanish dominions.
L'*Humble Chaumière*, No. 19, at St. Landry, (Louisiana.)
La *Triple Bienfaisance*, No. 20, at New-Orleans.
La *Sincère Amitié*, No. 21, at St. Martin-ville, Louisiana.)
Mobile Lodge, No. 22, at Mobile, (Alabama.)

(10)

EXPULSIONS.

Félix *Durousseau*, of Lodge No. 3, for malversation a Treasurer of said Lodge, & Joseph *Flee*, for conduc unworthy of a Mason.

John Lewis Francis *Chatry*, of Lodge No. 4, for non pay ment of his dues, & John Baptist *Cabos*, on account o immorality.

Joseph *Dorfeuil*; Manuel *Prados*,; Hyppolite *Meynard* de *Saffranque* & Manuel G. *Visoso*, of Lodge No. 5, for non payment of their dues.

MOST WOR∴ BROTHER,

Agreeably to the regulations of the Grand Lodge, I have the honour to forward to you one copy of the list of the Grand Officers for the masonic year 5823, & members of the same, together with the list of the expulsions which were communicated.

*With sentiments of high regard, I am
Most W∴ Brother,
Your devoted & affectionate Brother,*

Na. The Grand Secretary's Adress, is FRANCIS DISSARD, Esq.—New-Orleans.

GRAND LODGE

OF THE

Most Ancient & Honourable Fraternity of Free & Accepted Masons of Louisiana.

THE Grand Lodge of Louisiana having met a the hall of their sittings, in the City of New-Orleans, the 3d day of the 11th month A∴ L∴ 5823, the day of their Grand quartely Communication & the same having been opened in ample form, the election of the Grand Officers for the ensuing year was proceeded to & the brethren whose names follow were declared to be duly elected,

VIZ :

The M. W. B. John Francis Canonge,	R∴ W∴ Grand Master,
R. W. B. Yves Lemonnier,	Deputy Grand Master,
R. W. B. Lewis A. Faustin de Bodin,	Senior Grand Warden,
R. W. B. Amédée Longer,	Junior Grand Warden,
W. B. Francis Dissard,	Grand Secretary,
W. B. George W. Morgan,	Grand Treasurer,
W. B. Lewis Moreau Lislet,	Gd. Chaplain or Orator,
W. B. Christian Miltenberger, W. B. J. H. Holland,	} Grands Stwarts,
W. B. Charles L. Garnier,	Grand Sword-Bearer or Master of Ceremonies,
W. B. Peter Roche,	Grand Marshal,
W. B. James Vienne,	Grand Pursuivant.

(4)

And the 11th day of February, A∴ D∴ 1824, the day of the grand annual & general communication, the several Grand Officers elected were successively installed into their respective offices, agreeably to ancient usages; and after being duly proclaimed, they received the cordial & accustomed salutations of all the members present.

The new Grand Master appointed the following Grand Officers:

Brother Félix F. BRUNEL,   *Senior Grand Deacon*,
Stephen BERTEL   *Junior Grand Deacon*.

Committee of Correspondence.
The R. W. B.—D. F. BURTHE,
R. W. B.—A. LONGER,
R. W. B.—J. H. HOLLAND.

Committee of Accounts.
The R. W. B.—G. DEBUYS
R. W. B.—L. A. F. DE BODIN,
R. W. B.—J. VIENNE.

Committee of Information.
The R. W. B.—C. MILTENBERGER,
R. W. B.—L. DUHART,
R. W. B.—N. LESCONFLAIR.

Committee of Economy.
The R. W. B.—S. BERTEL,
R. W. B.—G. H. DE LEAUMONT,
R. W. B.—J. B. FAGET.

(5)

LIST OF THE MEMBERS OF THE GRAND LODGE OF THE STATE OF LOUISIANA.

GRAND OFFICERS.

The M. W. B. John Francis CANONGE, Counsellor at Law, R∴ A∴, K∴ T∴, *Grand Master,*

The R. W. B. Yves LEMONNIER, Doctor of Medecine, Past-Grand-Master, R∴ A∴, K∴ T∴, *Deputy Grand Master,*

The R. W. B. Lewis Alexander Faustin DE BODIN, an Officer of the Bank, R∴ A∴, *Senior Grand Warden,*

The R. W. B. Amédée LONGER, Merchant, R∴ A∴, K∴ T∴, *Junior Grand Warden,*

The R. W. B. Dominick Francis BURTHE, Gentleman, R∴ A∴ *Past-Grand-Master,*

The R. W. B. Francis DISSARD, formerly an Inabitant of St. Domingo, R∴ A∴, K∴ T∴, *Grand Secretary,*

The R. W. B. George W. MORGAN, Sheriff of the Parish of Orleans, R∴ A∴, *Grand Treasurer,*

The R. W. B. Lewis MOREAU LISLET, Counsellor at Law, Past-Grand-Master, R∴ A∴, K∴ T∴, *Grand Chaplain or Orator,*

The R. W. B. Félix F. BRUNEL, Clerk of Notary, R∴ A∴, *Senior Grand Deacon,*

The R. W. B. Stephen BERTEL, Architect, R∴ A∴, K∴ T∴, *Junior Grand Deacon,*

The R. W. B. Christ. MILTENBERGER, Doctor of Medecine, R∴ A∴,
The R. W. B. J. H. HOLLAND, Deputy Sheriff, R∴ A∴, K∴ T∴, } *Grand Stewars,*

(6)

The R. W. B. Charles L. GARNIER, Mercht. R∴ A∴ K∴ T∴, *Grand Sword-bearer or Master of Ceremonies,*

The R. W. B. Peter ROCHE, Printer, P∴ M∴, *Grand Marshal,*

The R. W. B. James VIENNE, Merchant, R∴ A∴, *Grand Pursuivant,*

Brother Francis CHABRAN, R∴ A∴, *Grand Tyler.*

Members of the Grand Lodge holding no Office in the same.

The R. W. B. Modeste LEFEBVRE, Merchant, Past-Grand Master, R∴ A∴, K∴ T∴.

The R. W. B. John SOULIE', Merchant, Past-Grand Master, R∴ A∴.

The R. W. B. Augustin MACARTY, Gentleman, Past-Grand Master, R∴ A∴, K∴ T∴.

The R. W. B. Gaspard DEBUYS, Merchant, Past-Deputy Grand Master, R∴ A∴.

The R. W. B. John Baptist LABATUT, Mercht. R∴ A∴.

The R. W. B. V. Amédée BONJEAN, Jeweller, R∴ A∴.

The R. W. B. Peter LARTIGUE MONGRUE', Officer in the Navy, R∴ A∴.

The R. W. B. Spire LOQUET, Professor of Languages, R∴ A∴.

The R. W. B. John Baptist FAGET, R∴ A∴, K∴ T∴.

The R. W. B. Bartholomew BACAS, Ebonist, P∴ M∴.

The R. W. B. John GUADIZ, Dentist, R∴ A∴, K∴ T∴.

The R. W. B. Anatole PEYCHAUD, Recorder & Justice of the Peace, R∴ A∴, K∴ T∴.

The R. W. B. Lewis DUHART, Professor of Languages, R∴ A∴.

The R. W. B. Lewis J. DUFILHO, Apothecary, R∴ A∴, K∴ T∴.

(7)

The R. W. B. Nicholas Lesconflair, Architect, R∴ A∴, K∴ T∴

The R. W. B. John Baptist Gilly, Merchant, R∴ A∴, K∴ T∴

The R. W. B. Nicholas Mioton, Confectionner, R∴ A∴

The R. W. B. Lewis Melchior Reynaud, R∴ A∴

The R. W. B. Hyppolite Doiron, Ebonist, R∴ A∴

The R. W. B. Manuel Fleitas, Gentleman, R∴ A∴, K∴ T∴

The R. W. B. Joseph Calixte Cougourdan, Architect, R∴ A∴, K∴ T∴

The R. W. B. John B. Plauche', Merchant, R∴ A∴

The R. W. B. Fréderic Letanneur, Mercht. R∴ A∴

The R. W. B. Philip Pedesclaux, Notary, R∴ A∴, K∴ T∴

The R. W. B. Gabriel Henry De Leaumont, an Officer of the Bank, R∴ A∴

The R. W. B. Bartholomew Grima, Mercht. P∴ M∴

The R. W. B. Francis Xavier Martinez y Pizarro, R∴ A∴, K∴ T∴

The R. W. B. H. R. Denis, Counsellor at law, R∴ A∴

The R. W. B. Charles Kroll, Officer in the Navy, R∴ A∴

The R. W. B. Bazile Beauregard, Mercht. P∴ M∴

The R. W. B. Peter A. Rousseau, gentleman, R∴ A∴

The R. W. B. Charles Maurian, Counsellor at Law, member of the general Assembly of the State of Louisiana, R∴ A∴, K∴ T∴

The R. W. B. Joseph Sanchez, Surgeon, R∴ A∴

The R. W. B. Peter Chevalier, Apothecary, R∴ A∴

The R. W. B. Francis J. Verrier Merchant, R∴ A∴

The R. W. B. René Lemonnier, Doctor of Medecine, R∴ A∴

The R. W. B. Peter Blanchard, Dentist, P∴ M∴

(8)

OFFICERS *Representing the several Lodges under the Jurisdiction of the Grand Lodge.*

No. 1, { D. F. BURTHE, — *Master,*
Edmond J. FORSTALL, Merch. R∴ A∴, *Senior Warden,*
Michel ANDRY, Inhabitant, R∴ A∴, *Junior Warden.*

No. 2, { Its Constitution has been withdrawn for not having met during one year.

No. 3, { M. FLEITAS, — *Master,*
Thomas BLOIS Jr. Merchant, R∴ A∴, *Senior Warden,*
John W. BINGEY, Inspector of the Custum-house, R∴ A∴, K∴ T∴, *Junior Warden.*

No. 4, { F. DISSARD, — *Master,*
P. CHEVALIER, — *Senior Warden,*
Raimond BLANCAND, Merchant, M∴, *Junior Warden.*

No. 5, { J. H. HOLLAND, — *Master,*
P. ROCHE, — *Senior Warden,*
J. B. FAGET, — *Junior Warden.*

No. 6, { Their Charter has been withdrawn by a resolution of the Grand Lodge.

No. 7, | Have returned their Charter.

No. 8, | No proxy.

No. 9, | Represented by Brother J. GUADIZ, their proxy.

No. 10, | Represented by Brother F. DISSARD, their proxy.

No. 11, | Have returned their Charter.

No. 12, | Represented by Brother J. F. CANONGE, their proxy.

No. 13, | Represented by Brother G. DEBUYS, their proxy.

No. 14, | The W. Master has returned its Charter.

No. 15, | Represented by Brother J. F. CANONGE, their proxy.

No. 16, | No proxy.

No. 17, | Represented by Brother J. F. CANONGE, their proxy.

No. 18, | No proxy.

No. 19, | Represented by Brother J. B. FAGET, their proxy.

(9)

No. 20, { Y. LEMONNIER, Master,
Lewis FOURCAND, Printer, M∴, Senior Warden,
Anthony BARBE, Merchant, M∴, Junior Warden.

No. 21, | Represented by Brother Y. LEMONNIER, their proxy.

No. 22, | No proxy.

No. 23, | Represented by Brother L. A. F. DE BODIN, their proxy.

No. 24, | Represented by Brother F. DISSARD, their proxy.

List of Lodges under the Jurisdiction of the Grand Lodge.

La Parfaite-Union, No. 1, sitting in the City of New Orleans.

La Concorde,   No. 3,   ditto.

La Persévérance, No. 4,   ditto.

L'Etoile Polaire, No. 5,   ditto.

Los Amigos Reunidos, No. 8, in the Spanish dominions.

La Réunion à la Virtud, No. 9,   ditto

L'Etoile Flamboyante, No. 10, at Bâton-Rouge, (Lna.).

La Vérité, No. 12, at Donalsonville, (Louisiana).

L'Union, No. 13, at Natchitoches, ditto.

Columbian, No. 15, at Alexandria, ditto.

Ewreka, No. 16, at Blakeley, State of Alabama.

Washington, No. 17, at Bâton-Rouge, (Louisiana).

La Aurora de Yucatan, No. 18, in the Spanish dominions.

L'Humble Chaumière, No. 19, at St. Landry, (Louisiana.

La Triple-Bienfaisance, No. 20, at New-Orleans.

La Sincère Amitié, No. 21, at St. Martinville, (Louisiana.

Mobile Lodge, No. 22, at Mobile, (Alabama).

L'Union, No. 23, Parish St. James, county of Acady.

Western-Star, No. 24, at Monroe, (Ouachita).

(10)

EXPULSIONS.

Felix DUROUSSEAU, of Lodge No. 3, for malversation as Treasurer of said Lodge, & Joseph FLKE, for conduct unworthy of a Mason.

John Lewis Francis CHATRY, of Lodge No. 4, for non payment of his dues, & John Baptist CANOS, on account of immorality.

Joseph DORFEUIL ;—Manuel PRADOS ;—Hyppolite MEYNARD de SALFRANQUE ;—Manuel G. VISOSO ; and in 1823,—Urbin MEILLEUR &—Michael MEILLEUR, of Lodge No. 5, for non payment of their dues.

———:◉:◉:◉———

MOST WOR∴ BROTHER,

Agreeably to the regulations of the Grand Lodge, I have the honour to forward to you one copy of the list of the Grand Officers for the masonic year 5823, & members of the same, together with the list of the expulsions which were communicated.

With sentiments of high regard, I am

Most W∴ Brother,

Your devoted & affectionate Brother.

Dinard G^d Sec^{ry}

No. The Grand Secretary's Adress, is FRANCIS DISSARD, Esq.—New-Orleans.

(11)

EXTRACT *of the proceedings of the R. W. Grand Lodge.*

16 *November* 1821.

Resolved—That this R. W. Grand Lodge does acknowledge as true and lawful Members of the great Mystic Family, all regular Masons whether of the rite of Ancient York, that of France (sometimes called modern Masonry) or that of Herodom of Scotland.

8*th February* 1822.

Resolved—That this R. W. Grand Lodge do grant a warrant of Constitution for the formation of a Lodge to be holden in the Parish of St. James under the title of the UNION Lodge No. 23.

15*th February* 1822.

Resolved—That the annual Catalogue of this R. W. Grand Lodge shall set forth the reasons for which the warrants of Constitution of several of the Lodges have been withdrawn.

15*th February* 1822.

Resolved—That a warrant of Constitution be granted for the formation of a Lodge to be holden at the town of Monroe, in the Parish of Ouachita under the title of the WESTERN STAR, No. 24.

30*th March* 1822.

Resolved—That in future it shall be the duty of the Grand Secretary to transmit annually to the Grand Lodges with which he corresponds a return of the last election with the sign manual of the six first Officers.

20*th September* 1823.

The committee to whom was refferred the communication from a number of members of the Society of Freemasons assembled at the Capitol in the City of Washington March 9th 1822, reported against the formation of a General Grand Lodge of the United States as recommended in the said communication.—*Resolved* that this right worshipful Grand Lodge do approve the reasons therein set forth and adopt the said report.

Ordered that the same be printed and a copy thereof forwarded to Brother WILLIAM W. SEATON at Washington and to each of the Grand Lodges of our correspondence.

January 3*d* 1824.

A communication was received informing the right worshipful Grand Master and Brethren that all differences which have heretofore existed between any of the Lodges under their jurisdiction have happily terminated and that the greatest harmony now prevails among the Brethren.

EXTRACT
of the
PROCEEDINGS
of the
GRAND LODGE
of the
Most Ancient Fraternity
OF FREE & ACCEPTED MASONS
of the
STATE OF LOUISIANA,
Held in the City of New-Orleans.

Published by order of the Society.

NEW-ORLEANS,

PRINTED BY BROTHER L. FOURCAND.

———:◎:———

A∴ L∴ 5824.—A∴ D∴ 1825.

MOST WOR∴ BROTHER,

Agreeably to the regulations of the Grand Lodge, I have the honour to forward to you one copy of the list of the Grand Officers for the masonic year 5825, & members of the same, together with the list of the expulsions which were communicated.

With sentiments of high regard, I am

Most W∴ Brother,

Your devoted & affectionate Brother,

Dissard   Gd. Sry.

N₀. The Grand Secretary's Adress, is FRANCIS DISSARD, Esq.—New-Orleans.

GRAND LODGE

OF THE

Most Ancient & Honourable Fraternity of Free & Accepted Masons of Louisiana.

THE Grand Lodge of Louisiana having met a the ha∴ of their sittings, in the City of New-Orleans, the 3d day of the 11th month A∴ L∴ 5824, & the same having been opened in ample form, the election of the Grand Officers for the ensuing year was proceeded to & the brethren whose names follow were declared to be duly elected, Viz :

The M. W. B. *John Henry* HOLLAND, - R∴ W∴ Grand Master,
R. W. B. *Lewis A. Faustin* DE BODIN, - Deputy Grand Master,
R. W. B. *Amédée* LONGER, - - - - - - - Senior Grand Warden,
R. W. B. *Charles* MAURIAN, - - - - - - Junior Grand Warden,
   W. B. *Francis* DISSARD, - - - - - - - Grand Secretary,
   W. B. *Christian* MILTENBERGER, - - Grand Treasurer,
   W. B. *Lewis* MOREAU LISLET, - - - Gd. Chaplain or Orator,
   W. B. *Nicholas* MIGTON, - - - - - - ⎱ Grands Stewarts,
   W. B. *Francis John* VERRIER, - - - ⎰
   W. B. *Peter* ROCHE, - - - - - - - - - - Grand Sword-Bearer or Master of Ceremonies,
   W. B. *Vincent* RAMOS, - - - - - - - - Grand Marshal,
   W. B. *Victor* DE ST. VICTOR, - - - - Grand Pursuivant.

(4)

And on the 9th day of the same month A∴ D∴ 1825, the day of the grand annual & general communication, the several Grand Officers elected were successively installed into their respective offices, agreeably to ancient usages; and after being duly proclaimed, they received the cordial & accustomed salutations of all the members present.

The new Grand Master appointed the following Grand Officers:

Brother *Augustus* Douce, Senior Grand Deacon,
　　James Vienne, Junior Grand Deacon.

Committee of Correspondence.
The R. W. B.—D. F. Burthe,
　　R. W. B.—A. Longer,
　　R. W. B.—A. Macarty.

Committee of Accounts.
The R. W. B.—G. Debuys,
　　R. W. B.—L. A. F. de Bodin,
　　R. W. B.—J. Vienne.

Committee of Information.
The R. W. B.—G. W. Morgan,
　　R. W. B.—Y. Lemonnier,
　　R. W. B.—G. H. de Leaumont.

Committee of Economy.
The R. W. B.—S. Bertel,
　　R. W. B.—J. B. Faget,
　　R. W. B.—A. Douce.

(5)

LIST of the Members of the Grand Lodge of the State of Louisiana.

GRAND OFFICERS.

The M. W. B. *John Henry* HOLLAND, Deputy Sheriff, R∴ A∴, K∴ T∴. *Grand Master.*

The R. W. B. *Lewis Alexander Faustin* DE BODIN, an Officer of the Bank, R∴ A∴ *Deputy Gd. Master.*

The R. W. B. *Amédée* LONGER, Merchant, R∴ A∴, K∴ T∴. *Senior Grand Warden.*

The R. W. B. *Charles* MAURIAN, Counsellor at Law, R∴ A∴, K∴ T∴. *Junior Grand Warden.*

The R. W. B. *John Francis* CANONGE, Counsellor at Law, R∴ A∴, K∴ T∴. *Past-Grand-Master.*

The R. W. B. *Francis* DISSARD, formerly an Inabitant of St. Domingo, R∴ A∴, K∴ T∴. *Grand Secretary.*

The R. W. B. *Christian* MILTENBERGER, Doctor of Medecine, R∴ A∴. *Grand Treasurer.*

The R. W. B. *Lewis* MOREAU LISLET, Counsellor at Law, Past-Grand-Master, R∴ A∴, K∴ T∴.
Grand Chaplain or Orator.

The R. W. B. *Augustus* DOUCE, Ebonist, R∴ A∴, K∴ T∴. *Senior Grand Deacon.*

The R W. B. *James* VIENNE, Merchant, R∴ A∴, K∴ T∴. *Junior Grand Deacon.*

The R. W. B. *Nicholas* MIOTON, Confectionner, R∴ A∴.
The R. W. B. *Francis John* VERRIER, Merchant, R∴ A∴. } *Grand Stewards:*

(6)

The R. W. B. *Peter* ROCHE, Printer & Bokseller, R∴ A∴ *Grand Sword bearer or Master of Ceremonies.*

The R. W. B. *Vincent* RAMOS, Gentleman, R∴ A∴ *Grand Marshal.*

The R. W. B. *Victor* DE ST. VICTOR, an Officer of the Bank, P∴ M∴ *Grand Pursuivant.*

Brother *Francis* CHABRAN, R∴ A∴ *Grand Tyler.*

Members of the Grand Lodge holding no office in the same.

The R. W. B. *Modeste* LEFEBVRE, Merchant, Past-Grand Master, R∴ A∴, K∴ T∴

The R. W. B. *John* SOULIE', Merchant, Past-Grand Master, R∴ A∴

The R. W. B. *Augustin* MACARTY, Gentleman, Past-Grand Master, R∴ A∴, K∴ T∴

The R. W. B. *Yves* LEMONNIER, Doctor of Medecine, Past-Grand Master, Past-Deputy Grand Master, R∴ A∴, K∴ T∴

The R. W. B. *Dominick Francis* BURTHE, Gentleman, Past-Grand Master, R∴ A∴

The R. W. B. *John Baptist* LABATUT, Mercht. R∴ A∴

The R. W. B. *Amédée* BONJEAN, Jeweller, R∴ A∴

The R. W. B. *Gaspard* DEBUYS, Merchant, R∴ A∴

The R. W. B. *George W.* MORGAN, Sheriff of the Parish of Orleans, R∴ A∴

The R. W. B. *Peter* LARTIGUE MONGRUE', Officer in the Navy, R∴ A∴

The R. W. B. *Spire* LOQUET, Professor of Languages, R∴ A∴

The R. W. B. *John Baptist* FAGET, R∴ A∴, K∴ T∴

The R. W. B. *Bartholomew* BACAS, Ebonist, P∴ M∴

(7)

The R. W. B. *John* Guadiz, Dentist, R∴ A∴, K∴ T∴.
The R. W. B. *Anatole* Peychaud, Marshal of the City of New Orleans, R∴ A∴, K∴ T∴.
The R. W. B. *Lewis* Duhart, Professor of Languages, R∴ A∴.
The R. W. B. *Joseph Calixte* Cougourdan, Architect, R∴ A∴, K∴ T∴.
The R. W. B. *Lewis Joseph* Dufilho, Apothecary, R∴ A∴, K∴ T∴.
The R. W. B. *Nicholas* Lesconflair, Architect, R∴ A∴, K∴ T∴.
The R. W. B. *Manuel* Fleitas, Gentleman, R∴ A∴, K∴ T∴.
The R. W. B. *Stephen* Bertel, Architect, R∴ A∴, K∴ T∴.
The R. W. B. *John B.* Plauche', Merchant, R∴ A∴.
The R. W. B. *Gabriel Henry* de Leaumont, an Officer of the Bank, R∴ A∴.
The R. W. B. *Francis Xavier* Matinez y Pizarro, R∴ A∴, K∴ T∴.
The R. W. B. *H. R.* Denis, Counsellor at law, R∴ A∴.
The R. W. B. *Charles* Kroll, Officer in the Navy, R∴ A∴.
The R. W. B. *Bazile* Beauregard, Merchant, M∴.
The R. W. B. *Peter* Blanchard, Dentist, M∴.
The R. W. B. *Peter Anthony* Rousseau, Gentleman, R∴ A∴, K∴ T∴.
The R. W. B. *Joseph* Sanchez, Surgeon, R∴ A∴.
The R. W. B. *Peter* Chevalier, Apothecary, R∴ A∴.
The R. W. B. *Charles L.* Garnier, Merchant, R∴ A∴, K∴ T∴.
The R. W. B. *Félix F.* Brunel, Clerk of Notary, R∴ A∴.
The R. W. B. *René* Lemonnier, Doctor of Medecine, R∴ A∴.

(8)

OFFICERS *Representing the several Lodges under the Jurisdiction of the Grand Lodge.*

No. 1, { J. B. PLAUCHÉ, - - - - - - - - - - - - - - - Master,
Manuel CRUZAT, R∴ A∴, - - - - - Senior Warden,
Victor DE ST. VICTOR, - - - - - - - - Junior Warden.

No. 3, { M. FLEITAS, - - - - - - - - - - - - - - Master,
John W. BINGEY, Inspector of the Custum-house, R∴ A∴, K∴ T∴, - - - Senior Warden,
Lewis CHAUVEAU, R∴ A∴, - - - - - - Junior Warden.

No. 4, { F. DISSARD, - - - - - - - - - - - - - - Master,
Peter LABARRERE, merchant, R∴ A∴, Senior Warden,
Joaquin VIOSCA, Merchant, R∴ A∴, - Junior Warden.

No. 5, { J. H. HOLLAND, - - - - - - - - - - - - - Master,
P. ROCHE, - - - - - - - - - - - - - - - Senior Warden,
J. B. FAGET, - - - - - - - - - - - - - - Junior Warden.

No. 8,—No proxy.
No. 9,—Represented by Brother J. GUADIZ, their proxy.
No. 10,—Represented by Brother F. DISSARD, their proxy.
No. 12,—Represented by Brother J. F. CANONGE, their proxy.
No. 13,—Represented by Brother G. DEBUYS, their proxy.
No. 15,—Represented by Brother J. F. CANONGE, their proxy.
No. 16,—No proxy.
No. 17,—Represented by Brother J. F. CANONGE, their proxy.
No. 18,—No proxy.
No. 19,—Represented by Brother J. B. FAGET, their proxy.

No. 20, { L. DUHART, - - - - - - - - - - - - - - - Master,
Anthony BARRE, Merchant, R∴ A∴, - Senior Warden,
B. Charles DUCHAMP, Mercht. R∴ A∴. Junior Warden.

No. 21,—Represented by Brother Y. LEMONNIER, their proxy.
No. 23,—Represented by Brother L. A. F. DE BODIN, their proxy.
No. 24,—Represented by Brother F. DISSARD, their proxy.

No. 25, { A. DOUCE, - - - - - - - - - - - - - - - Master,
V. RAMOS, - - - - - - - - - - - - - - - Senior Warden,
John COLSSON, M∴, - - - - - - - - - - Junior Warden.

(9)

LIST OF LODGES UNDER THE JURISDICTION OF THE GRAND LODGE.

La Parfaite-Union, No. 1, sitting in the City of New-Orleans.

La Concorde, No. 3, ditto.

La Persévérance, No. 4, ditto.

L'Etoile Polaire, No. 5, ditto.

Los Amigos Reunidos, No. 8, in the Spanish dominions.

La Réunion à la Virtud, No. 9, ditto.

L'Etoile Flamboyante, No. 10, at Bâton-Rouge, (Lna.).

La Vérité, No. 12, at Donalsonville, (Louisiana).

L'Union, No. 13, at Natchitoches, ditto.

Columbian, No. 15, at Alexandria, ditto.

Ewreka, No. 16, at Blakeley, State of Alabama.

Washington, No. 17, at Bâton-Rouge, (Louisiana).

La Aurora de Yucatan, No. 18, in the Spanish dominions.

L'Humble Chaumière, No. 19, at St. Landry, (Louisiana)

La Triple-Bienfaisance, No. 20, at New-Orleans.

La Sincère Amitié, No. 21, at St. Martinville, (Louisiana.

L'Union, No. 23, Parish St. James, county of Acady.

Western-Star, No. 24, at Monroe, (Ouachita).

Lafayette, No. 25, at New-Orleans.

(10)

EXPULSIONS *during the year* 1824.

Henry BEEBE, late one of the Wardens of Lodge No. 3, and a members of the Grand Lodge of this State, expelled by the Grand Lodge at the quarterl, communication 26th June 1824 for murder.

John NAVARRE, of Lodge No. 4, for non payment of his dues.

J. L. CHABERT, of Lodge No. 5, for non payment of his dues.

Joshua M. CLEAVLAND, of Lodge No. 15, for anti masonic conduct.

Théon BARBERET, of Lodge No. 20, for non payment of his dues

Extracts of the Deliberations of the R. W. Grand Lodge.

25th *September* 1824.

Resolved—That all the Masons who take the prison bounds be, and they are hereby suspended from their masonic fuctions, during the time they avail themselves of the protection of the laws relative to the said prison bounds.

6th *November*.

Resolved—That a warrant of Constitution be granted for the formation of a new Lodge in New-Orleans under the title of LAFAYETTE Lodge, No. 25.

GRAND ROYAL ARCH CHAPTER

Of the State of Louisiana.

At a meeting of the Grand Royal Arch Chapter of the State of Louisiana, held in ample form in the City of New Orleans, on the 22th day of the month of January, A. D. 1825, R. A. 2354, the said Grand Chapter was opened and it was proceeded to the election of the Grand Officers for this year and the brethren whose names follow, were duly elected, TO WIT:

J. H. HOLLAND,	Grand High Priest,
L. A. F. DE BODIN,	Deputy Grand High Priest,
A. LONGER,	Grand King,
S. BERTEL,	Grand Scribe,
F. DISSARD,	Grand Secretary,
C. MILTENBERGER,	Grand Treasurer,
C. MAURIAN,	Grand Chaplain or Orator,
P. ROCHE,	Grand Captain Royal Arch.

And on the 29th day in the same month and year, the said Grand Officers elect, were severally installed according to the ancient usages, into their respective offices and being duly proclaimed, they received the cordial and accustomed salutations of the brethren present.

(12)

A LIST of the members of the Grand Royal Arch Chapter of the State of Louisiana.

The M. E. *John Henry* HOLLAND, - - Grand High Priest,
The M. E. *Lewis A. Faustin* DE BODIN, Deputy Gd. high Priest,
The M. E. *Amédée* LONGER, - - - - - Grand King,
The M. E. *Stephen* BERTEL, - - - - - Grand Scribe,
The M. E. *John Francis* CANONGE, - Past Gd. High Priest,
The M. E. *Francis* DISSARD, - - - - - Grand Secretary,
The M. E. *Christ.* MILTENBERGER, Grand Treasurer,
The M. E. *Charles* MAURIAN, - - - - Gd. Chaplain or Orator,
The M. E. *Peter* ROCHE, - - - - - - - Grand Captain R. A.

Members of the Grand Chapter who are not in office.

The M. E. *Jonh* SOULIE', Past Grand High Priest,
The M. E. *Modeste* LEFEBVRE, Past Grand High Priest,
The M. E. *Yves* LEMONNIER, Past Grand High Priest,
The M. E. *Augustin* MACARTY, Past Grand High Priest,
The M. E. *Lewis* MOREAU LISLET, Past Grand High Priest,
The M. E. *Dominick Francis* BURTHE, Past Grand high Priest,
The M. E. *Joseph Calixte* COUGOURDAN,
The M. E. *Victor Amédée* BONJEAN,
The M. E. *Peter* LARTIGUE MONGRUE',
The M. E. *John Baptist* LABATUT,
The M. E. *Spire* LOQUET,
The M. E. *George W.* MORGAN,
The M. E. *Gaspard* DEBUYS,

(13)

The M. E. *John* GUADIZ,
The M. E. *Nicholas* MIOTON,
The M. E. *Nicholas* LESCONFLAIR,
The M. E. *Anatole* PEYCHAUD,
The M. E. *John Baptist* FAGET,
The M. E. *J. Manuel* FLEITAS,
The M. E. *Gabriel Henry* DE LEAUMONT,
The M. E. *Lewis Joseph* DUFILHO,
The M. E. *Lewis* DUHART,
The M. E. *H. R.* DENIS,
The M. E. *F. Xavier* MARTINEZ Y PIZARRO,
The M. E. *John Baptist* PLAUCHE,
The M. E. *James* VIENNE,
The M. E. *Charles L.* GARNIER,
The M. E. *Charles* KROLL,
The M. E. *René* LEMONNIER,
The M. E. *Félix F.* BRUNEL,
The M. E. *Peter* CHEVALIER,
The M. E. *Joseph* SANCHEZ,
The M. E. *Francis John* VERRIER,
The M. E. *Peter Anthony* ROUSSEAU,
The M. E. *Augustus* DOUCE,
The M. E. *Melchior* MALLEIM,
The M. E. *Vincent* RAMOS.

EXTRACT

OF THE

PROCEEDINGS

OF THE

GRAND LODGE

OF THE

Most Ancient Fraternity

OF

FREE AND ACCEPTED MASONS

OF THE

STATE OF LOUISIANA,

Held in the City of New-Orleans.

☞ *Published by order of the Society.* ☜

NEW-ORLEANS:

....
Printed by A. PEYCHAUD.
....
A∴ L∴ 5825—A∴ D∴ 1825.

Most Wor∴ Brother,

AGREEABLY to the Regulations of the Grand Lodge, I have the honor to forward you one copy of the List of the Grand Officers for the Masonic year 5826, and Members of the same, together with the List of Expulsions which were communicated.

With sentiments of high regard, I am

Most Wor∴ Brother,

Your devoted and affectionnate Brother,

[signature]
Gd. Sec'ry.

☞ The Grand Secretary's Address, is Fcis. Dissard, Esq. New-Orleans.

GRAND LODGE
of the
MOST ANCIENT AND HONOURABLE FRATERNITY
of
FREE AND ACCEPTED MASONS
of
LOUISIANA.

THE Grand Lodge of Louisiana having met at the hall of their sittings, in the City of New-Orleans, the 31st day of the 10th month A∴ L∴ 5825, and the same having been opened in ample form, the election of the Grand Officers for the ensuing year was proceeded to and the brethren whose names follow, were declared to be duly elected, viz :

J. H. HOLLAND,	R. W. Grand Master,
J. M. FLEYTAS,	Deputy ditto.
A. LONGER,	Senior Gd. Warden.
C. MAURIAN,	Junior ditto.
F. DISSARD,	Grand Secretary,
C. MILTENBERGER,	Grand Treasurer,
L. MOREAU LISLET,	Gd. Chaplain or Orator
N. MIOTON,	Grand Steward,
F. J. VERRIER,	ditto.
C. L. GARNIER,	Gd. Sword-Bearer or [Master of Ceremonies.

4

VINCENT RAMOS, - - - - - - - Grand Marshal,
J. C. COUGOURDAN, - - - - - - Gd. Pursuivant,

And on the 15th day of the 11th month A∴ L∴ 5825, the day of the grand annual and general communication, the several Grand Officers elected were successively installed into their respective offices, agreeably to ancient usages ; and after being duly proclaimed, they received the cordial and accustomed salutations of all the Members present.

The new Grand Master appointed the following Grand Officers :

A. DOUCE,   -   -   -   -   Senior Grand Deacon,
A. DUCROS,   -   -   -   -   Junior   ditto.

Committee of Correspondence.
D. F. BURTHE——A. LONGER——CHLS. MAURIAN.

Committee of Accounts.
J. M. FLEYTAS——L. A. F. de BODIN——J. VIENNE.

Committee of Information.
G. W. MORGAN—J. F. CANONGE—G. H. de Leaumont.

Committee of Economy.
S. BERTEL——J. B. FAGET——AUGUSTE DOUCE.

LIST of the Members of the Grand Lodge of the State of Louisiana.

J. H. HOLLAND, deputy sheriff, R∴ A∴ K∴ T∴ Gd. Master.

J. M. FLEYTAS, freeholder, Dep. G. M∴ R∴ A∴ K∴ T∴

A. LONGER, merchant, R∴ A∴ K∴ T∴ Senior Gd. Warden.

C. MAURIAN, counsellor at law, R∴ A∴ K∴ T∴ Junior Grand Warden.

J. F. CANONGE, counsellor at law, R∴ A∴ K∴ T∴ Past Grand Master.

F. DISSARD, formerly an inhabitant of St. Domingo, R∴ A∴ K∴ T∴ Grand Secretary.

C. MILTENBERGER, doctor of medecine, R∴ A∴ Grand Treasurer.

L. MOREAU LISLET, Counsellor at law, Past Grand Master, R∴ A∴ K∴ T∴ Grand Chaplain or Orator.

A. DOUCE, cabinet maker, R∴ A∴ K∴ T∴ Senior Grand Deacon.

A. DUCROS, freeholder, R∴ A∴ Junior Grand Deacon.

N. MIOTON, confectioner, R∴ A∴ Grand Steward.

F. J. VERRIER, merchant, R∴ A∴ Grand Steward.

C. L. GARNIER, R∴ A∴ Grand Sword bearer or Master of Ceremonies.

V. RAMOS, freeholder, R∴ A∴ Grand Marshal.

C. COUGOURDAN, R∴ A∴ K∴ T∴ Grand Pursuivant.

A. F. RENAULD, M∴ Grand Tyler.

Members of the Grand Lodge, holding no Office in the same.

M. LEFEBVRE merchant, Past Grand Master, R∴ A∴ K∴ T∴

J. SOULIE' merchant, Past Grand Master, R∴ A∴

A. MACARTY, freeholder, Past Grand Master, R∴ A∴ K∴ T∴

Y. LE MONNIER, doctor of medecine, Past Grand Master, Past Deputy Grand Master, R∴ A∴ K∴ T∴

D. F. BURTHE, freeholder, Past Grand Master, R∴ A∴

L. A. F. de BODIN, clerk in the bank, Ex-Deputy Grand Master, R∴ A∴

J. B. LABATUT, merchant, R∴ A∴
A. BONJEAN, jeweller, R∴ A∴
E. BERTEL, freeholder, R∴ A∴ K∴ T∴
G. DEBUYS, merchant, R∴ A∴
G. W. MORGAN, sheriff of the Parish of Orleans, R∴ A∴
S. LOQUET, professor of languages, R∴ A∴
J. B. FAGET, broker, R∴ A∴ K∴ T∴
B. BACAS, cabinet maker, P∴ M∴
J. GUADIZ, dentist, R∴ A∴ K∴ T∴
A. PEYCHAUD, marshal of the city of New-Orleans, R∴ A∴ K∴ T∴
L. J. DUFILHO, Jr. apothecary, R∴ A∴ K∴ T∴
N. LESCONFLAIR, architect, R∴ A∴ K∴ T∴
J. B. PLAUCHE', merchant, R∴ A∴
J. VIENNE, merchant, R∴ A∴ K∴ T∴
G. H. de LEAUMONT, an officer of the bank, R∴ A∴
P. ROCHE, book-seller, R∴ A∴
F. X. MARTINEZ Y PIZARRO, R∴ A∴ K∴ T∴
H. R. DENIS, counsellor at law, R∴ A∴
C. KROLL, officer in the navy, R∴ A∴
P. BLANCHARD, dentist, P∴ M∴
P. A. ROUSSEAU, freeholder, R∴ A∴ K∴ T∴
J. SANCHEZ, surgeon, R∴ A∴
P. CHEVALIER, apothecary, R∴ A∴
F. F. BRUNEL, clerk of notary, R∴ A∴
R. LEMONNIER, doctor of medecine, R∴ A∴
L. FOURCAND, printer, W∴ M∴
P. B. DUBAYLE, teacher of languages, W∴ M∴ of the Lodge No. 10.

Honorary Member.

G. M. GENERAL LAFAYETTE (general) R∴ A∴ K∴ T∴

Officers representing the several Lodges under the Jurisdiction of the Grand Lodge.

No. 1.
- J. B. PLAUCHE - - - - - Master,
- M. CRUZAT, R∴ A∴ - - Senior Warden,
- V. de St. VICTOR, - - - - Junior Warden,

No. 3.
- M. FLEYTAS, - - - - - Master,
- A. MORPHY, c. at law, R∴ A∴ Senior Warden,
- J. AUBERT, mcht. R∴ A∴ K∴ T∴ Jr. Warden,

No. 4.
- C. KROLL, - - - - - Master,
- A. BOURGEAU, engineer, R∴ A∴ Sr. Warden,
- A. BARBE, merchant, R∴ A∴ Junior Warden,

No. 5.
- J. H. HOLLAND, - - - - Master,
- J. B. FAGET, - - - - - Senior Warden,
- A. QUERTIER, M∴ - - - - Junior Warden,

No. 8.—Her charter taken from her.

No. 9.—Waiting for information.

No. 10.—Represented by F. Dissard, their proxy.

No. 12.—Represented by J. F. Canonge, their proxy.

No. 13.—Represented by G. Debuys, their proxy.

No. 15.—Represented by J. F. Canonge, their proxy.

No. 16.—Her charter taken from her for non payment of her [dues.

No. 17.—Represented by J. F. Canonge, their proxy.

No. 18.—Her charter taken from her for non payment of her [dues.

No. 19.—Represented by J. B. Faget, their proxy.

No. 20.
- L. FOURCAND, - - - - Master,
- M. J. DUCAYET, auctioneer, Senior Warden,
- A. HEBRARD, taylor, M∴ Junior Warden.

No. 21.—Represented by Y. Le Mounier, their proxy.

No. 22.—Her charter taken from her.

No. 23.—Represented by L. A. F. de Bodin, their proxy.

No. 24.—Represented by F. Dissard, their proxy.

No. 25.
- A. DOUCE, - - - - - Master,
- V. RAMOS, - - - - - Senior Warden,
- A. DUCROS, - - - - - Junior Warden.

LIST of Lodges under the Jurisdiction of the Grand Lodge.

La Parfaite-Union, No. 1, sitting in the city of New-Orleans.
La Concorde,	No. 3,	ditto.
La Persévérance, No. 4,	ditto.
L'Etoile Polaire, No. 5,	ditto.
La Reunion à la Virtud, No. 9, Spanish dominions.
L'Etoile Flamboyante, No. 10, at Baton-Rouge, (Louisiana.)
La Vérité, No. 12, at Donaldsonville, (Louisiana.)
L'Union, No. 13, at Natchitoches, ditto.
Columbian, No. 15, at Alexandrie, ditto.
Washington, No. 17, at Baton-Rouge, (Louisiana.)
L'Humble Chaumière, No. 19, at St. Landry (Louisiane.)
La Triple Bienfaisance, No. 20, at New-Orleans.
La Sincère Amitié, No. 21, at St. Martinsville (Louisiana.)
L'Union, No. 23, Parish St. James, county of Acadia.
Western Star, No. 24, at Monroe (Ouachita.)
Lafayette, No. No. 25, at New-Orleans.

Expulsions during the year 1825.

BAZILE BEAUREGARD, of the Lodge No. 20, for non-payment of his dues.

LE BARON, of the Loge No. 5.

REINSTALLED.

J. L. Chabert, of the Lodge No. 5.

EXTRACTS

Of the Deliberations of the R∴ W∴ Grand Lodge, during the year 1825.

SITTING OF FEBRUARY 19th.

On motion—Resolved that the following amendments to the general rules and regulations of the Grand Lodge be and the same are hereby adopted.

The Grand Lodge presided by the Grand Master and the other Grand Officers, is composed of all the founders of the Grand Lodge, of all the Past Masters who have been duly elected to preside in any of the Lodges of this jurisdiction, and who have or shall declare their intentions to remain permanent members of the Grand Lodge, of the brethren who had been Wardens of the several Lodges under our jurisdiction, previous to the election in the year of Masonry 5825, and who availed themselves of the privilege they then possessed of remaining members after their functions of Warden had expired by making application to that effect, and of the Representatives and Proxies of all the Lodges of the jurisdiction.

Resolved—That each of the Representatives and Proxies have the right of causing themselves to be represented in the Grand Lodge by a Brother of their Lodge who has held an office in the said Lodge, equal to the one held at the time by the Representative who sends the substitute. But the substitute is not entitled to fill the office of the Brother whose proxy he is if the said Brother should be an officer.

On each of the days of Grand Communication, all regular Masons to whatever degree they belong shall be admitted as visitor in the Grand Lodge.

If any of the Officers of this Grand Lodge, shall be absent for three meetings in succession, without assigning any reasons for his absence; such Officer shall be considered as having resigned his office.

SITTING OF FEBRUARY 7th.

On motion—Resolved, that a Masonic Festival shall be offered to our R.·. B.·. LAFAYETTE, whose arrival is announced in New-Orleans.

A Committee of Arrangement was appointed, and every necessary arrangement made, when in its sitting of April 14th 1825, the Colums being filled with more than three hundred Brethren, the R.·. B.·. Lafayette was introduced, and there received the most fraternal proofs of the respects which his virtues inspired; after which he assisted to a most splendid banquet, ordered by said Committee.

SITTING OF SEPTEMBER 24th.

Resolved—That no diploma will be delivered by the Grand Secretary, except after receiving payment for the same.

Resolved—That the Grand Lodge will co-operate with the other Grand Lodges in the United-States, for the erection of a monument to the memory of our M.·. W.·. B.·. GEORGE WASHINGTON, at Mount Vernont.

Resolved—That the Committee of Correspondance will open a Fraternal Communication with the Grand Lodges of England, Ireland, Scotland and France.

SITTING OF DECEMBER 31st.

Resolved—That a diploma shall be sent to our R.·. B.·. G. M. Lafayette, (General) as an honorary member of the Grand Lodge of the State of Louisiana.

GRAND ROYAL ARCH CHAPTER
OF THE
STATE OF LOUISIANA.

AT a meeting of the Grand Royal Arch Chapter of the State of Louisiana, held in ample form in the city of New-Orleans, (at Polar Star Lodge, No. 5, the ordinary place of its sittings) on the 28th day of the month of January, A∴ A∴ 1826, R∴ A∴ 2355, the said Grand Chapter was opened and it was proceeded to the Election of the Grand Officers for this year, and the Brethren whose names follow, were duly elected, TO WIT :

J. H. HOLLAND,	Grand High Priest,
J. M. FLEYTAS,	Dep. Gd. High Priest,
A. DOUCE,	Grand King,
E. BERTEL,	Grand Scribe,
J. F. CANONGE,	Ex-Gd. High Priest,
F. DISSARD,	Grand Secretary,
C. MILTENBERGER,	Grand Treasury,
C. MAURIAN,	G. Chaplain or Orator,
C. L. GARNIER,	Gd. Cap. Royal Arch,
J. F. PINSON,	Grand Captain of the [Hosts.

And on the 24th day of February, in the same year, the said Grand Officers elect, were severally installed according to the ancient usages, into their respective offices and being duly proclamed, they received the cordial and accustomed salutations of the Brethren present.

A LIST

Of the Members of the Grand Royal Arch Chapter of the State of Louisiana.

J. H. HOLLAND,	Grand High Priest,
J. M. FLEYTAS,	Deputy Grand High Priest,
A. DOUCE,	Grand King,
E. BERTEL, founder	Grand Scribe,
J. F. CANONGE,	Past Grand High Priest,
F. DISSARD,	Grand Secretary,
C. MILTENBERGER,	Grand Treasurer,
C. MAURIAN,	Grand Chaplain or Orator,
C. L. GARNIER,	Grand Captain R∴A∴
J. F. PINSON,	Grand Captain of the Hosts.

MEMBERS

Of the Grand Chapter who are not in Office.

J. SOULIE', founder	Past Grand High Priest.
M. LEFEBVRE, founder	ditto.
Y. LEMONNIER, founder	ditto.
A. MACARTY, founder	ditto.
L. MOREAU LISLET, founder	ditto.
D. F. BURTHE,	ditto.
L. A. F. de BODIN,	ditto.

J. C. COUGOURDAN, fdcr. | M. MALLEIM,
V. A. BONJEAN, founder, | A. LONGER,
J. B. LABATUT, founder, | S. LOQUET,
P. ROCHE, | G. DEBUYS,
G. W. MORGAN, | N. MIOTON,
J. GUADIZ, | P. M. A. PEYCHAUD,
N. LESCONFLAIR, | G. H. LEAUMONT,
J. B. FAGET, | H. R. DENIS,
L. J. DUFILHO, | J. B. PLAUCHE',
F. X. Martinez Y PIZARRO | C. KROLL,
J. VIENNE, | F. F. BRUNEL,
R. LEMONNIER, | J. SANCHEZ,
P. CHEVALIER, | P. A. ROUSSEAU.
F. J. VERRIER,

HONORARY MEMBER.

GILBERT MORTIMER LAFAYETTE, (General.)

14

A LIST of the Royal Arch Chapters under the Jurisdiction of the Grand [Royal] Arch Chapter of Louisiana, with the names of their Representatives or Proxies.

CHAPTERS.	Places of their Sittings.	Names of Representatives or Proxies.
Concord, No. 1.	New-Orleans.	J. M. Fleytas, G∴ P∴ J. F. Pinson, R∴ J. W. Bingey, S∴
Perseverance, No. 2.	New-Orleans.	C. Kroll, G∴ P∴ A. Bourgeau, R∴ M. Malleim, S∴
Polar Star, No. 3.	New Orleans.	J. H. Holland, H∴ P∴ E. Bertel, K∴ J. B. Faget, S∴
Perfect Union No. 4.	New-Orleans.	J. B. Plauché, H∴ P∴ M. Cruzat, K∴ P. A. Rousseau, S∴
Fraternal Union de Caridad, No. 5.	Havana.	F. Dissard, Proxy.
Consolation, No. 6	Matanzas.	J. Guadiz, Proxy.
Washington, No. 7	New-Orleans.	A. Douce, G∴ P∴ Barabino, R∴ P. Lacoste, S∴

M. E. BRETHREN,

Agreeably to the rules of the Grand Royal Arch Chapter of the State of Louisiana, I have the favor to forward to you a copy of the proceedings of the Grand Royal Arch Chapter, for the year 5826, with a List of its Members and Grand Officers.

I have the favor to be

Your most obedient and affectioned Brother

Grand Secretary.

The Address of the Grand Royal Chapter, is to
F. DISSARD, Esq.—New-Orleans.

EXTRACT

FROM THE

PROCEEDINGS

OF THE

GRAND LODGE

of the

Most Ancient Fraternity

OF

FREE & ACCEPTED MASONS

OF THE

STATE OF LOUISIANA,

Held in the City of New-Orleans.

Published by order of the Society.

NEW-ORLEANS.
Printed at Nº. 20, Conde Street.

1827.

Most W∴ B∴

  Agreeably to the Regulations of the Grand Lodge, I have the honor to forward you one copy of the List of the Grand Officers, for the Masonic year 5827, and Members of the same, together with the List of Expulsions which were communicated.
  With sentiments of high regard, I am,
Most Wor∴ Brother,
    Your devoted and affectionate Brother,

     F. DISSARD,
      Grand Secretary.

☞ The Grand Secretary's address, is—*Francis Dissard Esq.* New-Orleans.

GRAND LODGE

OF THE

Most Ancient and Honourable Fraternity

OF

FREE AND ACCEPTED MASONS

Of Louisiana.

———◆———

THE GRAND LODGE OF LOUISIANA having met at the hall of their sittings, in the City of New-Orleans, the 30th day of the 10th month A∴ L∴ 5826, and the same having been opened in ample form, the ELECTION of the Grand Officers for the ensuing year was proceeded to and the Brethren whose names follow, were declared to be duly elected, viz :

T∴ M∴ R∴ B∴

JOHN Hy. HOLLAND, - - R∴ W∴ Grand Master,
J. MANUEL FLEYTAS, - - Dep. Grand Master,
CHARLES MAURIAN, - - Senior Grand Warden,
ALONZO M. MORPHY, - Junior Grand Warden,
FRANÇOIS DISSARD, - - Grand Secretary.
CHRIST. MILTENBERGER, Grand Treasurer,
P. M. ANATOLE PEYCHAUD, Gd. Chaplain or Orator,
ETIENNE BERTEL, - - - Grand Steward,
FRAN. JEAN VERRIER, - ditto.

CHARLES L. GARNIER, - - Grand Sword Bearer, or Master of Ceremonies.
ALEXANDER PHILIPS, - - Grand Marshal,
J. CALIXTE COUGOURDAN, Gd. Pursuivant.

And on the 14th day of the 11th month, A∴ L∴ 5826, the day of the Grand Annual and General Communication, the several Grand Officers elected were successively installed into their respective offices, agreeably to ancient usages; and after being duly proclaimed, they received the cordial and accustomed salutations of all the Members present.

The new Grand Master appointed the following Grand Officers:

BARTOLOME' LOPEZ, - - - Senior Grand Deacon.
GUILLAUME A. MONTMAIN, - Junior Grand Deacon.

Committee of Correspondence:
C. MAURIAN,—D. F. BURTHE,—A. LONGER.

Committee of Accounts:
J. M. FLEITAS—P. M. A. PEYCHAUD—J. BARABINO.

Committee of Information:
G. W. MORGAN—F. CANONGE—A. PHILIPS.

Committee of Economy:
E. BERTEL—J. B. FAGET—E. FISKE.

LIST

Of the Members of the Grand Lodge of the State of Louisiana.

JOHN HENRY HOLLAND, deputy sheriff of the parish of Orleans, R∴ A∴, K∴ T∴, Grand Master.

J. MANUEL FLEITAS, freeholder, R∴ A∴, K∴ T∴, Deputy Grand Master.

CHARLES MAURIAN, lawyer, R∴ A∴, K∴ T∴, Senior Grand Warden.

ALONZO M. MORPHY, lawyer, R∴ A∴, Junior Grand Warden.

JEAN FRANCOIS CANONGE, lawyer, R∴ A∴, K∴ T∴, Ex-Grand Master.

FRANCOIS DISSARD, late inhabitant of St. Domingo, R∴ A∴, K∴ T∴, Grand Secretary.

CHRISTIAN MILTENBERGER, doctor of medicine, R∴ A∴, Grand Treasurer.

P. M. ANATOLE PEYCHAUD, lawyer, R∴ A∴ K∴ T∴, Grand Chaplain or Orator.

BARTOLOME' LOPEZ, M∴ Senior Grand Deacon.

GUILLAUME A. MONTMAIN, R∴ A∴, K∴ T∴, freeholder, Junior Grand Deacon.

ETIENNE BERTEL, freeholder, Founder, R∴ A∴, K∴ T∴, Grand Steward.

FRANCOIS JEAN VERRIER, merchant, R∴ A∴, Grand Steward.

CHARLES L. GARNIER, merchant, R∴ A∴, K∴ T∴, Grand Sword Bearer or Master of Ceremonies.

ALEXANDER PHILIPS, merchant, R∴ A∴, K∴ T∴, Grand Marshal.

JR. CALIXTE COUGOURDAN, architect, R∴ A∴ K∴ T∴, Grand Pursuivant.

ANTOINE FRANCOIS RENAULT, painter, P∴ M∴, Grand Tyler.

MEMBERS

Of the Grand Lodge, holding no office in the same.

JEAN SOULIE, merchant, Founder, Past Grand Master, R∴ A∴

LOUIS MOREAU LISLET, lawyer, Founder, Past Gd. Master, R∴ A∴, K∴ T∴

MODESTE LEFEBVRE, merchant, Founder, Past Grand Master, R∴ A∴, K∴ T∴

YVES LE MONNIER, doctor of medicine, Founder, Past Master, R∴ A∴, K∴ T∴

AUGUSTIN MACARTY, freeholder, Founder, Past Gd. Gd. Master, R∴ A∴, K∴ T∴

DOMINIQUE FRANCOIS BURTHE, freeholder, Past Gd. Master, R∴ A∴

L∴ ALEXANDRE FAUSTIN DE BODIN, Officer of the Bank, ex-deputy G∴ Master, R∴ A∴

AMEDEE LONGER, merchant, ex-Senior Grand Warden, R∴ A∴, K∴ T∴

JEAN BAPTISTE LABATUT, merchant, Founder, R∴ A∴

VICTOR AMEDE'E BONJEAN, goldsmith, Founder, R∴ A∴

GASPARD DEBUYS, merchant, R∴ A∴

GEORGE W. MORGAN, sheriff of the Parish of Orleans, R∴ A∴

JEAN BAPTISTE PLAUCHE', merchant, R∴ A∴

BARTHELEMY BACAS, cabinet maker, P∴ M∴

NICOLAS MIOTON, confectioner, R∴ A∴

LOUIS J. DUFILHO, apothecary, R∴ A∴, K∴ T∴

JEAN BAPTISTE FAGET, broker, R∴ A∴, K∴ T∴

JACQUES VIENNE, merchant, R∴ A∴, K∴ T∴

NICOLAS LESCONFLAIR, architect, R∴ A∴, K∴ T∴

GABRIEL HENRY DE LAUMONT, officer of the Bank, R∴ A∴

FRANCOIS XAVIER MARTINEZ Y PIZARRO, A∴, K∴ T∴

[7]

PIERRE ANTOINE ROUSSEAU, Custom-house officer, R∴ A∴, K∴ T∴.
H. B. DENIS, lawyer, R∴ A∴.
CHARLES KROLL, late navy officer, R∴ A∴.
PIERRE CHEVALIER, apothecary, R∴ A∴.
PIERRE BLANCHARD, dentist, P∴ M∴.
RENE' LEMONNIER, doctor of medicine, R∴ A∴.
PIERRE DUBAYLE, teacher of languages, R∴ A∴.
JOSEPH BARABINO, merchant, R∴ A∴ K∴ T∴.
ANTONIO DUCROS, planter, R∴ A∴.
DANIEL R. HOPKINS, merchant, late Master of the Lodge No. 13, P∴ M∴.
CELESTIN LAVERGNE, planter, late Master of the Lodge No. 19, R∴ A∴.
JEAN-BAPTISTE GILLY, merchant, R∴ A∴.

Honorary Member.

M. P. GILBERT MOTTIER LAFAYETTE, R∴ A∴, K∴ T∴.

Officers representing
THE LODGES UNDER THE JURISDICTION OF
THE GRAND LODGE.

N° 1.	J. B. PLAUCHE',	Master.
	MANUEL CRUZAT, Naval officer, R∴ A∴	Senior Warden
	V. ST. VICTOR, officer of the bank, P∴ M∴	Junior Warden
N° 3.	A. M. MORPHY,	Master.
	JN. FELIX PINSON, architect, R∴ A∴ K∴ T∴	Senior Warden
	H. C. CAMMACK, R∴ A∴	Junior Warden
N° 4.	ANTOINE BARBE, merchant, R∴ A∴	Master.
	JOAQUIN VIOSCA, merchant, R∴ A∴	Senior Warden
	J. B. BALTAZAR PLAUCHE', freehold. M∴	Junior Warden
N° 5.	J. H. HOLLAND,	Master.
	VICTOR DAVID, merchant, R∴ A∴	Senior Warden
	AUGUSTE LIAUTAUD, merchant, P∴ M∴	Junior Warden

N°. 9. — Not represented.
N°. 10. — F. DISSARD, their proxy.
N°. 12. — J. F. CANONGE, their proxy.
N°. 13. — G. DEBUYS, their proxy.

[8]

N°. 15. — J. F. CANONGE, their proxy.
N°. 17. — J. F. CANONGE, their proxy.
N°. 19. — J. B. FAGET, their proxy.

N°. 20. { Y. LE MONNIER, - - - Master.
         J. M. JOSEPH DUCAYET, auctioneer, M∴ Senior Warden
         ANTOINE HERBARD, tailor, - Junior Warden

N°. 21. — Y. LE MONNIER, their proxy.
N°. 23. — L. A. F. DE BODIN, their proxy.
N°. 24. — F. DISSARD, their proxy.

N°. 25. { A. DUCROS, R∴ A∴ - - Master.
         G. A. MONTMAIN, R∴ A∴ K∴ T∴ Senior Warden
         ANTHONY GUIROT, merchant, R∴ A∴ Junior Warden

N°. 26. { A. PHILIPS, - - - - Master.
         EBEN FISKE, merchant, R∴ A∴ - Senior Warden
         WM. A. SHELDON, apothecary, R∴ A∴ Junior Warden

N°. 27. { Jph. BARABINO, - - - - Master.
         B. LOPEZ, - - - - - Senior Warden
         NICOLAS BERTOLI, R∴ A∴ - Junior Warden

----◆◇◆----

LIST
Of Lodges under the jurisdiction of the GRAND LODGE.

La Parfaite Union, N°. 1, sitting in the city of New-Orleans.
La Concorde, N°. 3,   ditto.
La Persévérance, N°. 4,   ditto.
L'Etoile Polaire, N°. 5,   ditto.
La Réunion à la Virtud, N°. 9, Spanish country.
L'Etoile Flamboyante, N°. 10, at Baton-Rouge (Louisiana)
La Vérité, N°. 12, at Donaldsonville   ditto.
L'Union, N°. 13, at Natchitoches   ditto.
Columbian, N°. 15, at Alexandria   ditto.
Washington, N°. 17, at Baton-Rouge   ditto.
L'Humble Chaumière, N°. 19, at St. Landry   ditto.
La Triple-Bienfaisance, N°. 20, at New-Orleans,   ditto.
La Sincère Amitié, N°. 21, at St. Martinville,   ditto.
L'Union, N°. 23, Parish of St. James,   ditto.
Western-Star, N°. 24, at Monroe (Ouachita)   ditto.
Lafayette, N°. 25, at New-Orleans.   ditto.
Harmony, N°. 26,   ditto.   ditto.
La Numantina, N°. 27,   ditto.   ditto.
St. Alban, N°. 28, at Jackson,   ditto.

[9]

EXPULSIONS
During the year 1826.

FELIX F. BRUNEL; DOMINIQUE DUMAINE; AUGUSTE DAVEZAC DE CASTRA; MICHEL D. ESCLAVA; WARREN D. C. HALL; SAMUEL HARRISON & NATHANIEL JENKINS, of the Lodge No. 3, for non-payment of their dues.

JOSEPH SANCHEZ, of the Lodge No. 4, for non-payment of his dues, and for conduct unbecoming a mason.

JOSEPH BILLS, of the Lodge No. 4, for non-payment of his dues.

BARTHELEMI GRIMA, of the Lodge No. 5, for conduct unbecoming a mason.

AUGUSTUS ADOLPHE and DANIEL LITTLE, of the Lodge No. 24, for conduct unbecoming a mason.

EXTRACTS
Of the Deliberations of the R∴ W∴ Grand Lodge, during the year 1826.

SITTING OF THE 26TH OF MARCH.

Resolved, That a W∴ M∴ who will be desirous to receive the degree of P∴ M∴ shall be exempted to pay the amount of the dispense to the G∴ L∴

SITTING OF THE 1st OF JULY.

Resolved, That the Grand Lodge, as also the different Lodges under its jurisdiction, shall join the Procession of the citizens of New-Orleans, to assist to the Funeral Oration of our illustrious Brethren THOMAS JEFFERSON and JOHN ADAMS, Ex-Presidents of the United States, in order to pay the respect due to their memory.

Constitution delivered to install a W∴ Lodge, at New-Orleans, under the title of LA NUMANTINA, N°. 27.

SITTING OF THE 4TH OF NOVEMBER.

Ditto, ditto at Vermillonville, parish of Lafayette, county of Attakapas, in this State, under the tittle of LAFAYETTE LODGE.

[10]

SITTING OF THE 5th JANUARY 1827.

Constitution delivered to install a W∴ Lodge at Jackson, parish of East-Flíciana, in this State, under the tittle of St. Alban's Lodge, N°. 28.

SITTING OF THE 14th OF JANUARY 1827.

Resolved, That the Oration delivered this day, by the W∴ B∴ A. Peychaud, Grand Chaplain, shall be printed and made a part of our proceedings.

ORATION

Delivered by W∴ B∴ A. PEYCHAUD,

Grand Chaplain of the G∴ L∴ of the State of Louisiana, on the 14th of January, at the installation of the Grand Officers.

Most Worshipful Gd∴ Master, Gd∴ Officers,

AND YOU MY BRETHREN,

AT the moment when the Grand Masonic assembly of the State has been organised for the year which we have first entered upon, may I be allowed, Brethren of all the Lodges, assembled in the bosom of the Grand Lodge under which we hold, to congratulate you on the happy auspices under which we meet, on the appointments made to the different dignities, and on the prospect of happiness and prosperity which opens before us.

The Royal Art has made unceasing progress in this jurisdiction. The zeal, the ability and the talents of the Grand Master, have powerfully contributed to spread the light, and to give to the profane world, a high idea of our august mysteries. We have seen the subordinate Lodges filled with the most respectable citizens, we have seen various columns arise, fair and strong supporters of the building on which we all labour with so much zeal, success and unanimity. Worthy Brothers, zealous in the cause of masonry, flying from persecution and intolerance, have come to seek a refuge in this blessed land of liberty. Here they have founded temples, and, above the fear of being disturbed by a suspicious and pusilanimous government, they find themselves protected and encouraged in their noble task. Ah! in taking a view of the governments of the old world, how dear to us will be the liberal institutions under which we live—how deeply will we be penetrated with love, admiration and gratitude for the immortal founders of our independence. If they saved their country, by delivering it from an odious yoke, they are also entitled to be called the benefactors of the human race. Animated by a sentiment of humanity, a tender and active compassion for the evils which afflicted mankind, they have, in their writings, vindicated the natural rights of man and of opinion—they have proclaimed that those rights are inalienable and imprescriptible; thus raising, in all countries, an aspiration for liberty of thinking and writing, for free commerce and industry, for entire freedom of worship, for the abolition of torture and cruel punishments—they gave to the nations, the model of a government the best adapted to work their happiness—in a word, they have paved the way for the regeneration of all nations, by destroying religious and political prejudices, and by restoring to them a proper feeling of their own dignity, too long suppressed by their oppressors. A memorable conflict between two countries arose, the one defending the natural rights of man, the other supporting the impious doctrine which subjects those rights to prescription, to policy or to written conventions. This grand cause was pleaded before the tribunal of public opinion in the presence of all Europe. The rights of man were boldly sustained and developed, without restriction or reserve, in writings which freely circulated from the banks of the Neva to those of the Gundalquivir. These discussions penetrated into countries the most debased, and the most remote hamlets—the inhabitants of which were astonished to know that they possessed rights—they learned how to appreciate them, and were informed that other men had conquered or defended them.

This digression, my Brethren, into which I have been drawn, by my admiration for the founders of our independence, is not foreign to my subject. I was discoursing of the progress and prosperity of our order: And is it not to their glorious labours, to their sublime conceptions, that we owe this prosperity? Under the egis of their guardian institutions, the Brethren spread over the surface of our vast republic, have nothing to fear from intolerance and superstition: on the contrary, the most illustrious citizens, the highest in office, are proud to belong to the great masonic family.

Our European Brethren do not enjoy the same degree of security. Religious and political prejudices, the spirit of intolerance and persecution seem again to revive to work the misery of mankind. Suspicious and pusilanimous governments have conceived a hatred for our order, so peaceful in its principles, so tranquil in its labours—and already, the tyranny of priests, fit auxiliary of kings, is striving to destroy our venerable institution. But should the throne and the altar, conspiring together, succeed in closing the temples and arresting the noble career of the children of light, still, the triumph of masonry, the reign of reason and liberal ideas, will only be deferred. We all feel that the human race can never return to its ancient barbarism.

If we take a view of the present state of Europe, we shall see that the principles of our immortal constitution are acknowledged by all enlightened men; we shall find them too widely diffused, too loudly professed, for the united efforts of tyrants and priests to hinder them from gradually penetrating the mass of the people and teaching them their rights. Yes, my Brethren, let us accord our belief to the prophetic words of a great orator (*) "The day will come, when li"berty, reigning without a rival in the two worlds, will realize "the wish of philosophy, will cleanse mankind of the crime "of war and proclaim universal peace; then the happiness "of the people will be the sole object of legislators, the sole "force of laws, the only glory of governments. Then pri"vate passions, converted into public virtues, will no longer "tear asunder the bonds of fraternity by their sanguinary "quarrels—that fraternity which ought to unite all govern"ments and all men—Then, finally, will be consummated "the pact of union between the whole human family."

This charming idea of a brotherly union of the whole human family, which no national or political interest would have force to disturb, is perhaps a vision; but a vision consoling to philosophy! In the midst of political discord, arising from the struggle of the oppressed against tyranny even in the enlightened age in which we live, the friend of humanity cannot taste unmixed pleasure, but by yielding himself to the pleasing hopes of futurity.

As for us, my Brethren, let us enjoy, with gratitude to the Almighty, all the blessings he has bestowed upon us. Let us continue to deserve the public esteem; let us persevere in spreading the light—and, casting its rays from all the altars of happy America, may it become a vast beacon, to direct the nations of the earth on the road to happiness and liberty.

(*) Mirabeau.

GRAND
ROYAL ARCH CHAPTER,

OF THE

STATE OF LOUISIANA.

AT a meeting of the GRAND ROYAL ARCH CHAPTER OF THE STATE OF LOUISIANA, held in ample form in the city of New-Orleans, on the 27th day of the month of January, A∴ D∴ 1827, R∴ A∴ 2356, the said Grand Chapter was opened and it was proceeded to the Election of the Grand Officers, for this year, and the Brethren whose names follow, were duly elected, to wit:

M∴ I∴ F∴ C∴

J. H. HOLLAND,	Grand High Priest.
J. M. FLEYTAS,	Dep. Gd. High Priest.
F. LE MONNIER,	Grand King.
M. CRUZAT,	Grand Scribe.
F. DISSARD,	Grand Secretary.
C. MILTENBERGER,	Grand Treasurer.
P. DUBAYLE,	Grand Orator.
J. F. PINSON,	Gd. Captain R∴ A∴
A. PHILIPS,	Gd. Captain of the hosts

And on the 3d day of February, in the same year, the said Grand Officers elect, were severally installed according to the ancient usages, into their respective offices and being duly proclaimed, they received the cordial and accustomed salutations of the Brethren present.

[15]

A LIST

OF THE MEMBERS OF THE GRAND CHAPTER OF THE STATE OF LOUISIANA.

JEAN HENRY HOLLAND, Grand High Priest,
J. MANUEL FLEYTAS, Dep. Grand High Priest
YVES LE MONNIER, founder, Grand King,
MANUEL CRUZAT, Grand Scribe,
J. FRANCOIS CANONGE, Ex-Grand High Priest
FRANCOIS DISSARD, Grand Secretary,
GHRISTIAN MILTENBERGER, Grand Treasurer,
PIERRE DUBAYLE, Grand Orator,
J. FELIX PINSON, G∴ Captain R∴ A∴
ALEXANDER PHILIPS, Gd. Captain of the hosts.

MEMBERS

Of the Grand Chapter who are not in Office.

J. SOULIE', founder, ancient Grand High Priest,
L. MOREAU LISLET, founder, ditto.
M. LEFEBVRE, founder, ditto.
A. MACARTY, founder, ditto.
D. F. BURTHE, ancient Grand High Priest,
L. A. F. DE BODIN, Ex-Deputy Grand High Priest,
E. BERTEL, founder,
J. C. COUGOURDAN, founder,
V. A. BONJEAN, founder,
J. B. LABATUT, founder,

G. W. MORGAN,   G. DEBUYS,
A. LONGER,   J. B. PLAUCHE',
J. B. FAGET,   P. M. A. PEYCHAUD,
C. L. GARNIER,   P. A. ROUSSEAU,
C. MAURIAN,   N. MIOTON,
L. J. DUFILHO JR.   H. R. DENIS,
P. X. MARTINEZ Y PIZARRO, G. H. DE LEAUMONT,
J. VIENNE,   F. J. VERRIER,
N. LESCONFLAIR,   C. KROLL,
M. MALLEIM,   J. BARABINO,
R. LE MONNIER,   C. LAVERGNE,
P. CHEVALIER,   R. D. HOPKINS.

HONORARY MEMBER :
M. P. GILBERT MOTTIER LAFAYETTE,

A LIST

Of the Royal Arch Chapters, under the Jurisdiction of the Grand Chapter of Louisiana, with the names of their Representatives or Proxies.

CHAPTERS.	PLACES OF THE SITTINGS.	REPRESENTATIVES.
LA CONCORDE, N°. 1.	N.-Orleans	A. M. Murphy, G. P. C. Miltenberger, K. C. L. Garnier, S.
LA PERSEVERANCE N°. 2.	N.-Orleans.	A. Barbe, G. P. F. Dissard, K. A. Bourgeau, S.
L'ETOILE POLAIRE N°. 3.	N.-Orleans	J. H. Holland, G. P. E. Bertel, K. F. J. Verrier, S.
PARFAITE UNION, N°. 4.	N.-Orleans.	J. B. Plauché, G. P. M. Cruzat, K. P. A. Rousseau, S.
WASHINGTON, N°. 7.	N.-Orleans.	Jh. Barabino, G. P. Pierre Lacoste, K. J. L. Thielen, S.

M∴ I∴ F∴ C∴

Agreeably to the rules of the Grand Royal Arch Chapter of the State of Louisiana, I have the favor to forward to you a copy of the proceedings of the Grand Royal Arch Chapter, for the year 5827, with a List of its Members and Grand Officers.

I have the favor to be
  Your most obedient and affectioned Brother.

      DISSARD,
       Grand Secretary.

NOTA.—*The Address of the Grand Royal Arch Chapter is to:* F. DISSARD, Esq. New-Orleans.

EXTRACT

FROM THE

PROCEEDINGS

OF THE

GRAND LODGE OF THE

MOST ANCIENT FRATERNITY

OF FREE AND ACCEPTED MASONS

OF THE

STATE OF LOUISIANA,

HELD IN THE CITY OF NEW-ORLEANS.

PUBLISHED BY ORDER OF THE SOCIETY.

New-Orleans:
PRINTED BY EDWIN LYMAN.
1828.

Most W∴ B∴

Agreeably to the Regulations of the Grand Lodge, I have the honor to forward you one copy of the list of the Grand Officers, for the Masonic year 5828, and Members of the same, together with the List of Expulsions which were communicated.

With sentiments of high regard, I am,
  Most Wor∴ Brother,
   Your devoted and affectionate Brother,
        F. DISSARD,
         Grand Secretary.

The Grand Secretary's address, is—FRANCIS DISSARD, Esq. New-Orleans.

GRAND LODGE

OF THE

Most Ancient and Honorable Fraternity

OF

FREE AND ACCEPTED MASONS

OF LOUISIANA.

THE GRAND LODGE OF LOUISIANA having met at the hall of their sittings, in the city of New-Orleans, 29th day of the 10th month A∴ L∴ 5827, and the same having been opened in ample form, the election of the grand officers for the ensuing year was proceeded to, and the brethren whose names follow, were declared to be duly elected, viz:

T∴ M∴ R∴ B∴

JOHN HENRY HOLLAND,	R∴ W∴ Grand Master,
ALONZO MORPHY	Deputy Grand Master,
CHARLES MAURIAN,	Senior Grand Warden,
AMEDÉE LONGER,	Junior Grand Warden,
FRANCOIS DISSARD,	Grand Secretary,
CHRISTIAN MILTENBERGER,	Grand Treasurer,
P. M. ANATOLE PEYCHAUD,	Gd. Chaplain or Orator,
J. B. FAGET,	Grand Steward,
FRAN. JEAN VERRIER,	Ditto.
CHARLES L. GARNIER,	Grand Sword Bearer, or Master of Ceremonies,
ALEXANDER PHILIPS,	Grand Marshal,
J. CALIXTE COUGOURDAN,	Gd. Pursuivant.

4

And on the 13th day of the 11th, month A∴ L∴ 5827, A∴ D∴ 1828, the day of the Grand Annual and General Communication, the several Grand Officers elected were successively installed into their respective offices, agreeably to ancient usages; and after being duly proclaimed, they received the cordial and accustomed salutations of all the Members present.

The new Grand Master appointed the following Grand Officers:

ETIENNE BERTEL, - - - - - - Senior Grand Deacon
GUILLAUME A. MONTMAIN, - - Junior Grand Deacon

Committee of Correspondence:
A. MORPHY, C. MAURIAN, A. PHILIPS.

Committee of Accounts:
A. PEYCHAUD, J. BARABINO, F. DISSARD.

Committee of Information:
Y. LE MONIER, G. W. MORGAN, J. B. Bzar. PLAUCHÉ.

Committee of Economy:
E. BERTEL, J. B. FAGET, J. GUERIN.

LIST OF THE MEMBERS
OF THE GRAND LODGE OF THE STATE OF LOUISIANA.

JOHN HENRY HOLLAND, deputy sheriff of the parish of Orleans, R∴ A∴, R∴ M∴, S∴ M∴, K∴ T∴, Grand Master.

ALONZO MORPHY, attorney at law, R∴ A∴, S∴ M∴, Deputy Grand Master.

CHARLES MAURIAN, lawyer, R∴ A∴, K∴ T∴, Senior Grand Warden.

AMEDÉE LONGER, merchant, R∴ A∴, K∴ T∴, Junior Grand Warden.

JEAN FRANCOIS CANONGE, lawyer, R∴ A∴, K∴ T∴, Ex-Grand Master.

FRANCOIS DISSARD, late inhabitant of St. Domingo, R∴ A∴, S∴ M∴, K∴ T∴, Grand Secretary.

PIERRE DUBAYLE, teacher of languages, R∴ A∴, S∴ M∴, K∴ T∴, Assistant Grand Secretary.

CHRISTIAN MILTENBERGER, doctor of medicine, R∴ A∴, Grand Treasurer.

P. M. ANATOLE PEYCHAUD, lawyer, R∴ A∴, K∴ T∴, Grand Chaplain, or Orator.
ETIENNE BERTEL, R∴ A∴, K∴ T∴, Senior Grand Deacon.
GUILLAUME A. MONTMAIN, R∴ A∴, S∴ M∴, K∴ T∴, freeholder, Junior Grand Deacon.
JEAN BAPTISTE FAGET, broker, R∴ A∴, K∴ T∴, Grand Steward.
FRANCOIS JEAN VERRIER, merchant, R∴ A∴, Grand Steward.
CHARLES L. GARNIER, merchant, R∴ A∴, S∴ M∴, K∴ T∴, Grand Sword Bearer or Master of Ceremonies.
ALEXANDER PHILIPS, merchant, R∴ A∴, S∴ M∴, C∴ T∴, Grand Marshal.
JOSEPH CALIXTE COUGOURDAN, architect, R∴ A∴, K∴ T∴, Grand Persuivant.
ANTOINE FRANCOIS RENAULT, painter, E∴ M∴, M∴ Grand Tyler.

MEMBERS OF THE GRAND LODGE,
HOLDING NO OFFICE IN THE SAME.

JEAN SOULIÉ, merchant, Founder, Past Grand Master, R∴ A∴.
LOUIS MOREAU LISLET, lawyer, Founder, Past Gd. Master, R∴ A∴, K∴ T∴.
YVES LE MONIER, doctor of medicine, Founder, Past Grand Master, R∴ A∴, K∴ T∴.
AUGUSTIN MACARTY, freeholder, Founder, Past Grand Master, R∴ A∴, K∴ T∴.
DOMINIQUE FRANÇOIS BURTHE, freeholder, Past Grand Master, R∴ A∴.
J. MANUEL FLEITAS, freeholder, Ex-Deputy Grand Master, R∴ A∴, K∴ T∴.
Lt. ALEXANDRE FAUSTIN DE BAUDIN, Officer of the Bank, R∴ A∴, S∴ M∴.
JEAN BAPTISTE LABATUT, merchant, Founder, R∴ A∴.
VICTOR AMEDÉE BONJEAN, goldsmith, Founder, R∴ A∴.
GEORGE WASHINGTON MORGAN, sheriff of the Parish Orleans, R∴ A∴.
JEAN BAPTISTE PLAUCHÉ, merchant, R∴ A∴.
BARTHELEMY BACAS, cabinet maker, P∴ M∴.
NICOLAS MIOTON, confectioner, R∴ A∴.
LOUIS J. DUFILHO, apothecary, R∴ A∴, K∴ T∴.
JACQUES VIENNE, merchant, R∴ A∴, K∴ T∴.
NICOLAS LESCONFLAIR, architect, R∴ A∴, K∴ T∴.

GABRIEL HENRY DE LEAUMONT, officer of the Bank R∴ A∴
FRANCOIS X. MARTINEZ Y PIZARRO, R∴ A∴ K∴ T∴
PIERRE ANTOINE ROUSSEAU, Custom-house officer, R∴ A∴, K∴ T∴
H. R. DENIS, lawyer, R∴ A∴
CHARLES KROLL, late navy officer, R∴ A∴
PIERRE CHEVALIER, apothecary, R∴ A∴
PIERRE BLANCHARD, dentist, P∴ M∴
RENE LE MONIER, doctor of medicine, R∴ A∴
JEAN BAPTISTE GILLY, merchant, R∴ A∴
JOSEPH BARABINO, merchant, R∴ A∴ S∴ M∴, K∴ T∴
ANTONIO DUCROS, planter, R∴ A∴
DANIEL R. HOPKINS, merchant, Past Master of the Lodge No. 13, R∴ A∴
CELESTIN LAVERGNE, planter, Past Master of the Lodge No. 19, R∴ A∴
ANTOINE BARBE, merchant, R∴ A∴, S∴ M∴

Honorary Member.

M. P. GILBERT MOTTIER LAFAYETTE, R∴ A∴, K∴ T∴

OFFICERS REPRESENTING THE LODGES
UNDER THE JURISDICTION OF THE GRAND LODGE.

No. 1.
- D. F. BURTHE, — W. Master,
- ANTOINE DUPUY, Past Master, R∴ A∴ — Senior Warden,
- FELIX FORMENTO, M. D. — Junior Warden.

No. 3.
- A. MORPHY, — W. Master,
- THOMAS BLOIS, merchant, R∴ A∴ — Senior Warden,
- BARTHELEMY FLEITAS, freeholder, R∴ A∴, S∴ M∴ — Junior Warden.

No. 4.
- J. B BALTAZAR PLAUCHE, freeholder, R∴ A∴, S∴ M∴ — W. Master,
- JOAQUIN VIOSCA, merchant, R∴ A∴ — Senior Warden,
- BAPTISTE AZERETE, Merchant, M∴ — Junior Warden.

No. 5.
- J. H. HOLLAND, — W. Master,
- E. BERTEL, — Senior Warden,
- J. J. BOUCHET RIVIERE, M. D. R∴ A∴, S∴ M∴ — Junior Warden.

No. 9. —Not represented.
No. 10. —F. DISSARD, Proxy.
No. 12. —J. F. CANONGE, Proxy.
No. 13. —C. MILTENBERGER, Proxy.
No. 15. —J. F. CANONGE, Proxy.
No. 17. —Charter withdrawn.
No. 19. —J. B. FAGET, Proxy.

7

No. 20.	Y. LE MONIER,	W. Master,
	ANTOINE HEBRARD, merchant tailor, M∴	Senior Warden,
	AMBROISE DUVAL, miniature painter, M∴	Junior Warden.
No. 21.	—Charter withdrawn.	
No. 23.	—L. A. F. DE BODIN, Proxy.	
No. 24.	—P. DISSARD, Proxy.	
No. 25.	G. A. MONTMAIN,	W. Master,
	J. ANTHONY GUIROT, merchant, R∴ A∴	Senior Warden,
	FRANCOIS DUBUC, druggist, E∴ A∴	Junior Warden.
No. 26.	SETH W. NYE, inspector of revenue, R∴ A∴, S∴ M∴	W. Master,
	COTTON HENRY, commission merchant R∴ A∴	Senior Warden,
	W. R. FALCONER, druggist, R∴ A∴, S∴ M∴	Junior Warden
No. 27.	JUAN GUERIN, broker, M∴	W. Master,
	LINO DE LA ROSA, merchant, M∴	Senior Warden,
	JUAN JOSE RICO, merchant, M∴	Junior Warden.
No. 28.	—J. H. HOLLAND, Proxy.	
No. 29.	—J. H. HOLLAND, Proxy.	
No. 30.	—J. H. HOLLAND, Proxy.	

LIST OF THE LODGES

UNDER THE JURISDICTION OF THE GRAND LODGE.

La Parfaite Union, N°. 1, sitting in the city of New-Orleans.
La Concorde, N°. 3, ditto.
La Persévérance, No. 4, ditto.
L'Étoile Polaire, N°. 5, ditto.
La Réunion à la Virtud, N°. 9, Spanish country.
L'Étoile Flamboyante, No. 10, at Baton-Rouge, (Louisiana.)
La Vérité, No. 12, at Donaldsonville, ditto.
L'Union, N°. 13, at Natchitoches, ditto.
Columbian, N°. 15, at Alexandria, ditto.
L'Humble Chaumière, N°. 19, at St. Landry, ditto.
La Triple Bienfaisance, No. 20, at New-Orleans, ditto.
L'Union, N°. 23, Parish of St. James, ditto.
Western-Star, N°. 24, at Monroe, (Ouachita) ditto.
Lafayette, N°. 25, at New-Orleans, ditto.
Harmony, N°. 26, ditto. ditto.
La Numantina, N°. 27, ditto. ditto.
St. Alban, N°. 28, at Jackson, ditto
Harmony, N°. 29, Opelousas, ditto.
Lafayette, N°. 30, at Vermilionville, (Attakapas) ditto.

8

EXPULSIONS DURING THE YEAR 1827.

WILLIAM HAYDEN, by Lodge N°. 15, non-payment of dues.
LEWIS DAVIS, by Lodge N°. 23, anti-masonic conduct.
BERNARD SYLVA, by Lodge N°. 25, ditto.

EXTRACTS

Of the Deliberations of the Grand Lodge of the State of Louisiana, during the year 1827.

SITTING OF THE 31st MARCH.

The 80th paragraph 1st section of chapter 2d of the general regulations amended.

Resolved, That whereas the lodges of the jurisdiction, have but one stated meeting per month, and as that part of the general regulations as it now exists, tends to embarrass their labors, the said lodges are authorized to receive at any and all of the meetings, petitions for affiliation and initiations.

SITTING 7th APRIL.

Resolved, That the grand master when re-elected, shall be re-installed into office by his predecessor if present, and in his absence, by the oldest past master present.

AMENDMENT TO THE GENERAL REGULATIONS.

Resolved, That from and after the 1st day of July 1827, the different lodges of this jurisdiction, shall not receive any visiter whatever, unless he shall exhibit a diploma in due form, from his lodge or from the grand lodge to whose jurisdiction he belongs, unless he shall be recommended and vouched for by known and worthy brethren. This regulation is not to exempt visiters from the accustomed examination, which shall hereafter be made with the most rigid strictness.

It is further resolved, That this amendment shall be immediately notified to all the lodges of the jurisdiction, and communicated to the grand lodges with whom this grand lodge is in correspondence.

Resolved, That henceforth, masons who have resided in the city of New-Orleans, for more than six months and who belong to no lodge of this state, shall not be admitted as visiters more than three times in any of the lodges of this jurisdiction; and the said lodges are hereby authorized to refuse admittance to any brother who comes within the meaning of this resolution.

9

It is further resolved, That the grand lodge will permit however the lodges to dispense with this rule in favor of any particular brother whom they may deem worthy.

SITTING 30th JUNE.

AMENDMENT TO THE GENERAL RULES.

Resolved, That in future, in order to be duly elected to the four first offices of the grand lodge, it shall be necessary to obtain an absolute majority of the votes of all the members present.

SITTING 9th MARCH, 1828.

Constitution granted to Feliciana Lodge, No. 31, to be located at St. Francisville, in this state.

CEREMONY OF LAYING THE FOUNDATION STONE

OF THE NEW-ORLEANS MARINER'S CHURCH.

Special Meeting of the Grand Lodge of the State of Louisiana, Sunday the 23d March, A. L. 5828, A. D. 1828.

The Grand Lodge met in the hall of the Polar Star Lodge (its usual place of sitting) at the hour of half past 11 o'clock, A. M. and was opened by the Grand Master in ample form. The brethren having been informed from the chair, that the object of the meeting, was the laying of the Corner Stone of the New-Orleans Mariner's Church, the rules for the forming and conducting the procession, were read by the Grand Secretary and committed to brother Alexander Philips, Esq. Grand Marshal. The necessary cautions were then given by the Grand Master and the Grand Lodge adjourned.

A procession was then formed, under the direction of the grand marshal, by brother George W. Boyd, companions Eben Fiske and L. Fleitas, and sir-knights George H. Hunter, F. L. White, and Alexander M'Connel, assistant grand-marshals, agreeably to the order published in the Louisiana Advertiser.

Good order prevailed during the whole time. The procession was headed by a fine battalion of United States' troops, under the command of colonel Taylor, to whose politeness the Grand Lodge is much indebted. Next came a respectable number of ship-masters, captains of Steam-boats, and mariners; after them, the several incorporated societies, public bodies, and authorities; and in the rear several hundred Masons, decorated with the insignia of their respective grades, and bearing with them the banners of

2

the various orders with their several mottos and devices, which with the brilliant costumes of the brethren, gave the finest appearance to the scene.

In this order the procession, accompanied by two bands of musick, moved up Rampart street to Toulouse street, down that street to Chartres street, up Chartres street to Custom-House street, thence through Custom-House and Bourbon streets to Canal street, where it halted opposite the dwelling of the Rev. Mr. Hull, until it was joined by that respectable clergyman and the Rev. Theodore Clapp, who, accompanied by J. A. Maybin and James Foster, Esqrs. of the building committee, were conducted by the grand marshal, and placed by the side of the grand chaplain. The procession then resumed its movement, and proceeded to the scite of the edifice, where it again halted—the ranks opened to the right and left, when the grand master, with the invited guests, and the officers and members of the grand lodge, passed through the line under the triumphal arch, and were received by the president and directors of the church society, on the platform which had been erected for the occasion, and took their seats. The masonic fraternity, the United States troops, mariners and citizens, who formed the residue of the procession, also passed through the arch to their station.

The day was fine, and nature seemed in harmony with the occasion of this assembling. Before the arrival of the procession, the custom-house, which had been opened for their accommodation, was filled with ladies. The large space within the railings around that building, contained several thousand spectators, who had assembled to witness the ceremony.

Silence having been proclaimed by the grand marshal, and repeated by the heralds attendant on the grand master, and by each of the grand marshals assistants, brother, the Reverend Theodore Clapp, of the Presbyterian church, and Chaplain of Harmony Lodge No. 25, rose at the request of the grand master, and addressed the throne of grace in a fervent and eloquent prayer, after which solemn music was played by the band.

J. A. Maybin, Esq. then made an appropriate address to the grand Master, on behalf of the directors, informing him of the object of the new building, and presenting him with the implements used by the fraternity (the plumb, square, level and compasses) and concluded by requesting that he would proceed and ascertain the fitness of the stone, and if it met his approbation, that he would be pleased to lay it according to the ancient usages of the order of Free Masonry.

The grand master replied that on behalf of the masons of this state, he accepted with pleasure the invitation of the directors—that as Masons, their profession enjoined upon them to be aiding and assisting in the erection of temples to the glory of our Supreme Grand Master—to charity—and to benevolence; and that it afforded them much happiness to be called upon, on the present occasion, to participate in the foundation of an institution having for its object the worship of our Creator, and the moral, religious, and temporal improvement of a most valuable and interesting portion of our fellow men.

The grand master then descended to the place where the stone was suspended, accompanied by the deputy grand master, the grand wardens and grand officers—by his excellency Henry Johnson, governor of the state; the honorable Peter Derbigny, secretary of state; the honorable A. Beauvais, president of the senate; the honorable François X. Martin, judge of the supreme court; the honorable Joseph Roffignac, mayor of the city; general W. L. Robeson; colonel G. W. Morgan, sheriff; the honorable Isaac A. Smith, and the honorable Philemon Thomas, senators, and François Gardere, Esq. state treasurer; the honorable S. S. Wheeler, and the honorable L. Thibodeau, members of the house of representatives, and all members of the masonic fraternity—col. Taylor, major Twiggs, captain Kerr, and several other officers, brethren, and citizens. The grand master having first applied his implements to the stone, said—"I pronounce this Foundation Stone of the Mariner's Church, to be well formed, true and trusty." The music then sounded a flourish, and Pleyel's Hymn was played by the band.

Brother J. P. Dubayle, Esq. acting for the grand treasurer (who was absent from indisposition) by the grand master's command, deposited in the cavity of the basement stone, a box containing several coins of the age, a beautifully wrought silver plate (the workmanship of Mr. Harland) on which was the following inscription:

"This Corner Stone of the New-Orleans Mariners' Church, was laid by JOHN HENRY HOLLAND, *most worshipful Grand Master of Masons for the state of Louisiana, on Sunday the 23d day of March, anno lucis 5828, anno domini, 1828,* assisted by Alonzo Morphy, right worshipful Deputy Grand Master, Charles Maurian, right worshipful Senior Grand Warden, Amadie Longer, right worshipful Junior Grand Warden, and the officers and members of the Grand Lodge of the said state of Louisiana, the officers and members of the subordinate Lodges in the city of New-Orleans, and a large and respectable number of sojourning Brethren."

And on the reverse:

"John Quincy Adams, President of the United States of America; Henry Johnson, Governor of the State of Louisiana; Joseph Roffignac, Mayor of the city of New-Orleans.

"Beverly Chew, President of the New-Orleans Mariner's Church Society; Samuel M'Cutcheon, Vice-President; Richard Relf, Treasurer; Hugh Farrie, Recording Secretary.

12

"*Directors*—J. W. Smith, D. Sheldon, H. Babcock, James Foster, J. A. Maybin, W. Christy, W. W. Caldwell, C. Paulding, R. M. Welman, J. Colles, R. Davidson.

"Architect, Joseph Pilie; Builders, T. Gardner, P. S. Hamblet, J. Chase.

"NEW-ORLEANS, MARCH 23d, 1828."

The box also contained the holy Bible, the constitution of the United States, and that of the state of Louisiana; the constitution of the Grand Lodge of Louisiana; the *Manuel Maçonnique, à l'usage des Franc-Maçons Acceptés du Rite Ancien d'York, résidants à la Louisiane. Par un Ancien Vénérable*; the order of procession; Paxton's Directory; the newspapers of the day, and a list of the members of the Grand Lodge, and of Polar Star, No. 5. The stone was thereupon lowered down into its place by three steps, the band playing an appropriate air.

The grand master then struck the stone three times with his mallet, and pronounced. "May the Grand Architect of the universe grant a blessing on this foundation stone which we have now laid, and enable us to finish this and all our works here below with his approbation, and then have our translation from this earthly abode to the heavenly temple above, there to enjoy light glory and bliss ineffable. Glory to God on High. Response by the brethren—as it was in the beginning, is now, and ever shall be. AMEN."

The *Cornucopia*, and the vessels containing the wine and oil, were brought from the platform by their bearers, and delivered, the *Cornucopia* to the deputy grand master, and the wine and oil to the grand wardens, who in successive order handed them to the grand master; by whom their contents were poured upon the stone, saying: "May the all bounteous Author of nature bless the inhabitants of this place with all the necessary comforts and conveniences of life; assist in the erection and completion of this building; protect the workmen against every accident; and long preserve this structure as a monument of the enlightened philanthrophy and benevolence of its founders; and may we at all times be granted the needed supply of the Corn of Nourishment, the Wine of Refreshment, and the Oil of Joy."

The grand master then addressed the grand chaplain, brother A. Peychaud, Esq. and said: "Have we here the first and greatest light in masonry?" He replied, "It is in my hand, most worshipful." "What instruction does it furnish us on the present occasion?"

The grand chaplain then read the following select passages from the holy writings:

"Thus sayeth the Lord God—behold, I lay in Zion, for a foundation, a Stone—a tried Stone—a PRECIOUS corner Stone—a new foundation. Judgment, also, will I lay to the Line, and Righteousness to the Plummet." Isaiah, xxviii. 16, 17.

13

"For behold the Stone which I have laid before Joshua. Upon one Stone shall be seven eyes. Behold, I will engrave the engraving thereof, sayeth the Lord of Hosts." Zach. iii. 9.

"Bless ye the Lord, all ye servants of the Lord. Lift up your hands in the Sanctuary and bless the Lord. The Lord that made Heaven and Earth bless ye, out of Zion." Psalms, cxxxiv.

GRAND HONORS BY THE MASONS.

The Grand Master then delivered the working tools to brother Joseph Pilie, Architect; and addressed him in the French language, as follows:

Mon Frère,

"Les administrateurs de l'Eglise des Marins ayant la plus grande confiance dans vos talents et dans votre fidélité, vous ont chargé de la surintendance des travaux de ce nouvel Edifice, qui doit être érigé à la gloire du Grand Architecte de l'Univers, et dont nous venons de poser la première Pierre. Tous ceux qui vous connaissent se félicitent d'avance, certains que vous vous acquitterez avec honneur de cet emploi important."

"Je vous présente donc avec plaisir, les outils dont vous devez vous servir dans vos travaux : ils réunissent à tout ce qui est nécessaire pour exercer votre profession, plusieurs Emblêmes Maçonniques. J'ai rempli mon devoir en les remettant entre vos mains. Puissiez-vous faire de ces instrumens un usage convenable, et vous rappeler qu'ils sont les symbôles des devoirs que la société impose à l'homme : elle attend de lui qu'il règle ses actions par le fil-aplomb de l'équité, qu'il tienne ses passions dans le cercle décrit par le Compas de la Vertu, et que son ambition ne s'élève jamais au-dessus du niveau d'une juste émulation, afin qu'arrivé au terme de la vie il puisse ressembler à un tabernacle bâti des matériaux les plus purs, par les mains des meilleurs ouvriers et que son âme, lorsque ces matériaux tomberont en poussière semblable à cette Pierre angulaire, reste ferme et de niveau, par l'effet des vertus Maçonniques, qui sont la Charité, l'Amour Fraternel, et une Bienveillance Universelle pour tous les hommes, et que nous devons tous pratiquer en secret."

To which Brother Pilie replied :

Très Illustre Grand-Maitre,

"Je reçois ces outils avec le respect que je vous dois, et la gratitude qu'a fait naitre en moi la confiance dont m'honorent les Administrateurs de l'Eglise des Marins. Je n'épargnerai rien pour m'aquitter de mon emploi à l'entière satisfaction de ceux qui me l'ont confié, et tandis que je ferai usage de ces instruments comme Architecte pratique, j'aurai présent à ma pensée les leçons morales dont ils sont les symboles."

All parties then returned to their stations on the platform, and an air was played by the band, after which the Reverend James F. Hull, agreeably to previous invitation, rose and delivered an oration. The music then struck up, "Come let us prepare," &c. and the procession moved in due form to the dwelling of brother Alexander Philips, Esq. who had politely offered the use of his elegant house for that purpose, and the Grand Lodge was closed in harmony.

GRAND ROYAL ARCH CHAPTER
OF THE STATE OF LOUISIANA.

At a meeting of the Grand Royal Arch Chapter of the State of Louisiana, held in ample form in the city of New-Orleans, on 26th day of the month of January, A∴ D∴ 1828, R∴ A∴ 2357, the said Grand Chapter was opened, and it was proceeded to the election of the grand officers, for this year, and the brethren whose names follow, were duly elected, to wit:

M∴ E∴ C∴

J. H. HOLLAND,	Grand High Priest.
A. MOHPHY,	Deputy Grand High Priest.
Y. LE MONIER,	Grand King.
D. F. BURTHE,	Grand Scribe.
F. DISSARD,	Grand Secretary.
C. MILTENBERGER,	Grand Treasurer.
P. DUBAYLE,	Grand Orator.
A. PHILIPS,	Grand Captain of the host.
J. BARABINO,	Grand Captain R∴ A∴.

And on the 9th day of March, in the same year, the said grand officers elect, were severally installed according to the ancient usages, into their respective offices, and being duly proclaimed, they received the cordial and accustomed salutations of the brethren present.

A LIST OF THE MEMBERS
OF THE GRAND CHAPTER OF THE STATE OF LOUISIANA.

JOHN HENRY HOLLAND,	Grand High Priest.
ALONZO MORPHY,	Deputy Grand High Priest.
YVES LE MONIER,	Grand King.

15

D. FRANCOIS BURTHE,   *Grand Scribe.*
J. FRANCOIS CANONGE,   *Ex-Grand Priest.*
FRANCOIS DISSARD,   *Grand Secretary.*
CHRISTIAN MILTENBERGER,   *Grand Treasurer.*
PIERRE DUBAYLE,   *Grand Orator.*
ALEXANDER PHILIPS,   *Grand Captain of the host.*
JOSEPH BARABINO,   *Grand Captain R∴ A∴*

MEMBERS OF THE GRAND CHAPTER
WHO ARE NOT IN OFFICE.

J. SOULIÉ, founder, Past Grand High Priest.
L. MOREAU LISLET, founder,   ditto.
M. LEFEBVRE, founder,   ditto.
A. MACARTY, founder,   ditto.
D. F. BURTHE,   ditto.
J. M. FLEITAS, Ex-Deputy Grand High Priest.
J. C. COUGOURDAN, founder,
V. A. BONJEAN,   ditto.
J. B. LABATUT,   ditto.
E. BERTEL,   ditto.

L. A. F. DE BODIN,	J. B. PLAUCHE,
G. W. MORGAN,	P. M. A. PEYCHAUD,
A. LONGER,	P. A. ROUSSEAU,
M. CRUZAT,	N. MIOTON,
J. B. FAGET,	H. R. DENIS,
G. L. GARNIER,	G. H. DE LEAUMONT,
C. MAURIAN,	F. J. VERRIER,
L. J. DUFILHO,	C. KROLL,
F. X. MARTINEZ Y PIZARRO,	J. B. GILLY,
J. VIENNE,	C. LAVERGNE,
N. LESCONFLAIR,	R. D. HOPKINS,
M. MALLEIM,	A. BARBE,
R. LE MONIER,	A. DUCROS,
P. CHEVALIER,	G. A. MONTMAIN.

HONORARY MEMBER:

M. P. GILBERT MOTTIER LAFAYETTE.

16

A LIST OF THE ROYAL ARCH CHAPTERS,

Under the Jurisdiction of the Grand Chapter of Louisiana, with the names of their Representatives or Proxies.

CHAPTERS.	PLACES OF THE SITTINGS.	REPRESENTATIVES.
LA CONCORDE, No. 1.	New-Orleans.	A. MORPHY, High Priest, C. MILTENBERGER, King, A. PHILIPS, Scribe.
LA PERSEVERANCE, No. 2.	New-Orleans.	J. B. PLAUCHE', High Priest, F. DISSARD, King, A. BOURGEAU, Scribe.
L'ETOILE POLAIRE, No. 3.	New-Orleans.	J. B. HOLLAND, High Priest, R. BERTEL, King, F. J. VERRIER, Scribe.
PARFAITE UNION, No. 4.	New-Orleans.	D. F. BURTHE, High Priest, M. CRUZAT, King, A. DUPUY, Scribe.
WASHINGTON, No. 7.	New-Orleans.	G. A. MONTMAIN, High Priest, A. DUCROS, King, A. F. GUIROT, Scribe.
LODGE OF MARK MASTERS,	Nachitoches.	B. LEONARD, R. W. Master, ST. AMAND, Senior Warden, LEWIS, Junior Warden.

COUNSEL OF ROYAL AND SELECT MASTERS, under the title of HOLLAND COUNSEL, No. 1; sittings in New-Orleans.
ENCAMPMENT OF THE SIR KNIGHTS TEMPLARS, under the title of the INDIVISIBLE FRIENDS, No. 6; sittings in New-Orleans.

M∴ E∴ C∴

Agreeably to the rules of the Grand Royal Arch Chapter of the State of Louisiana, I have the favor to forward to you a copy of the proceedings of the Grand Royal Arch Chapter, for the year 5828, with a list of its Members and Grand Officers.
    I have the favor to be
        Your most obedient and affectionate Brother.
                DISSARD,
                    Grand Secretary.

NOTA.—*The Address of the Grand Royal Arch Chapter is to:* F. DISSARD, Esq. New-Orleans.

EXTRACT

FROM THE

PROCEEDINGS

OF THE

GRAND LODGE

OF FREE AND ACCEPTED MASONS

OF THE

STATE OF LOUISIANA,

HELD IN THE CITY OF NEW-ORLEANS.

PUBLISHED BY ORDER OF THE SOCIETY.

NEW-ORLEANS:
PRINTED BY BUISSON & BOIMARE,
Conde-Street.

1830.

Most W∴ B∴.

Agreeably to the Regulations of the Grand Lodge, I have th[e] honor to forward you one copy of the list of its Grand Officers, an[d] members for the year 1830, with some resolutions and amendmen[ts] together with a list of the expulsions which have been communicate[d]

With sentiments of high regard, I am,
Most Wor∴ Brother,
Your devoted and affectionate Brother,

F. DISSARD,
Grand Secretary.

GRAND LODGE
OF
FREE AND ACCEPTED MASONS
OF LOUISIANA.

The Grand Lodge of Louisiana having met at the hall of their sittings, in the city of New-Orleans, 2d day of the 11th month A. L. 5829, and the same having been opened in ample form, the election of the grand officers for the ensuing year was proceeded to, and the brethren whose names follow, were declared to be duly elected, viz:

T∴ M∴ R∴ B∴

JOHN HENRY HOLLAND,	R. W. Grand Master.
AMEDEE LONGER,	Deputy Grand Master.
MARC FOUCHE' COUGOT,	Senior Grand Warden.
JN. BAPTISTE FAGET,	Junior Grand Warden.
F. DISSARD,	Grand Secretary.
LOUIS H. FERAUD,	Grand Treasurer.
ANATOLE PEYCHAUD,	Gd. Chaplain or Orator.
F. JEAN VERRIER,	Grand Steward.
FREDERIC BUISSON,	Ditto.
SAMUEL S. RELF,	Grand Sword bearer, or Master of Ceremonies.
J. A. ROCA Y SANTI PETRI,	Grand Marshal.
SETH W. NYE,	Grand Pursuivant,

And on the 10th day of January, A. D. 1830, the day of the Grand Annual and General Communication, the several Grand Officers elected were successively installed into their respective offices, agreeably to ancient usages; and after being duly proclaimed, they received the cordial and accustomed salutations of all the members present.

4

The New Grand Master appointed the following Grand Officers:

ADOLPHE W. PICHOT, - - - Senior Grand Deacon.
SAMUEL D. DIXON, - - - Junior Grand Deacon.

Committee of Correspondence.
D. F. BURTHE, A. LONGER, A. MORPHY.

Committee of Accounts.
G. W. MORGAN, C. L. GARNIER, A. PHILIPS.

Committee of Information.
M. F. COUGOT, J. B. FAGET, L. H. FERAUD.

Committee of Economy.
F. J. VERRIER, F. BUISSON, G. A. MONTMAIN.

The W. B. Grand Orator being absent, the W. B. Feraud, Grand Treasurer, delivered the following speech, at the request of the M. W. Grand Master.

I will not detain you a moment, my Brethren, in expatiating on the difficulty of the task with which I am charged nor on the insufficiency of my means for its suitable accomplishment; our M. W. Grand Master, has called upon me to fill the place of our absent Grand Orator, and in obeying that call, I trust to your indulgence. Masonry, from time immemorial, has been defined by our most enlightened brothren, the study of the sciences and the practice of virtue. After this definition of which each of you are prepared to acknowledge the exactitude, is it not permitted to us to boast of the utility and excellence of the R. Art.

Its object is to render man happy; and what surer means are there of obtaining it, than those which it employs: to enlighten the mind by instruction, and to form the heart by example, is not this the object of our labors, of our work: Is it not the meaning of the mystery which has been discovered to you, in every degree to which you have been advanced. The wisdom of the G. A. gave and executed the plan of this sublime institution; strength supports and preserves it and beauty adorns and embellishes it; it is in vain that envy and wikedness would endeavor to subvert the edifice raised on these three pillars, in vain will calumny direct its poisoned arrows against it; its origin is lost in the obscurity of time, and its end will be closed but with that of ages.

What do these enemies object to our order! if you assemble but to do good, say some of them, why make use of the mystery which envelops your meetings; do you believe, say others, that you are the only well informed, the only virtuous order of men; to wind up, again; others pretend that if the mystery can have been useful in times now past, it is at the present day perfectly useless and often injurious.

5

Let us not, my brethren, be embarrassed or dejected by these idle clamours.

They reproach us with the mystery and the secrets which veil our meetings from the gaze of the profane; But, can the truth, that light which the mason desires and seeks after, be without danger exposed to all? If I held shut up in my hand all the truths, said the learned Fontenelle, I would take good care not to open it. Wise and philosophic thought! All those who have studied and obtained a knowledge of man, have been obliged to concur in opinion that all truths are not useful and that several might easily become dangerous if unveiled to weak minds. It is then reserved but to some, to be in a condition, without risk, to obtain a knowledge of all truths; well then the mystery by its wisely directed experiments serves to ascertain what quantity of light may be imparted to each without dazzling him with it. Such has always been the cause of the discretion, of which the mason contracts the obligation from his entrance into the T∴. We read in a manuscript discovered by the famous Locke, the original of which appears to have been written by Henry the 6th, who reigned in England en 1436 " that masons have at all times, and from time to time communicated to mankind such of their secrets as might be useful to them and keeping back only those which might be prejudicial in bad hands, those which be or could be of no benefit to others and those which serve to bind the fraternity more firmly together." But these very secrets do not; exclusively belong to any particular family, or particular people; the order is as universal as the cause which gave rise to it. The only recommandations necessary for admission to our labours are moral qualifications; distinctions and advancement belong but to merit; it is here that true equality reigns, the emblem of which decorates the collar of the senior warden; not that brutal equality that breaks all the bonds of society by refusing to acknowledge any authority; but that wise and charitable equality which cause us to consider all men as brothers of the same origin, participating of the same nature and destined to the same end.

We find, again, in the manuscript already quoted, the answer to other objections of our enemies! we therein find this question " are masons better informed than other men? " and then follows the answer: " they have only the right and the opportunities of knowing more than other men, but many want capacity and a still greater number the vigilance and aptitude necessary to the acquirement of knowledge; and to this other question: " Are masons better than other men? " The answer is: " That some masons are not so virtuous as other men, but they are better than they would be if they were not masons. "

Is it not useless to answer those who wish to cause the mystery to be considered as dangerous; such a calumny is too absurd to require serious attention; and indeed, that a jealous despot who considers men but as victims devoted to his passions, sees not without uneasiness an association, whose chief end is to render all men happy; that the obligations and the oaths which masons take to be faithful to the government of their country, are not sufficient to remove the fears of the tyrant and that in his mischievous delirium he proscribes and persecutes them, we may easily conceive.

The perverse man cannot ascertain or appreciate the sacrifices which virtue knows how to impose, and besides the sight of a virtuous man acts as a reproach to him, which ruffles and puts him in a state of fury.

But, that this objection has been made in a republic, and in what Republic! In that, of which the fondamental basis seems to have had its source in the Masonic Code. In that of which the firm and liberal government leaves to man the exercise of all his liberty without converting it into licentiousness and gives to authority all the force and power due to a law, without its being able to convert it to despotism. What! could our republic have any thing to fear from those who at their meetings, after having paid that homage to the G∴ A∴ of the U∴ which is due to him and sought a benediction upon them and their works, have no other care, no other occupation than that of seeking after the means of assuring the happiness of their fellow men! No, no, let not yourselves be deceived, it is not for the safety of the republic that these enemies of the mystery tremble; for rather are these enemies of the mystery the enemies of the republic. They well know that so long as freemen assemble in their T∴, that they support wisdom, strength and beauty, where power is given to those who bear on their breast the emblem of the virtues which are in their hearts, equity, equality and rectitude, so long as they shall be conducted by the three great lights which impart to us our intelligence: morality, equity and moderation, in a word, so long as there shall exist Masons, the American Republic will have devoted and constant supporters.

As to the inutility, which is offered as a reproach to our institution, the ignorant man or the man of bad faith can alone attempt to suggest it. Experience proves to us that by a whimsical destiny of the human mind, the best things degenerate by making them too general; would not that cause suffice for rendering obvious the necessity of an association more especially consecrated for the preservation of the deposit of human knowledge and for giving an example of the virtues; and our society being at the same time a private society where none are admitted but those whose virtue render them worthy and a general association where none but the wicked are excluded, ought it not to be considered as an institution the most fit to fulfill that useful mission. Give to a certain class of men this sacred deposit, would it not be lost when that class might be dispersed; it was confided to the Bramins and disappeared with them; the Priests of Memphis assumed the keeping of it, but it was buried under the ruins of the Egyptian priesthood, its lot was the same at Eleusis. A like inconvenience exists when it is intrusted to one nation; most powerful people have by turns been effaced from the surface of the earth and their sciences have disappeared with them; but the religious system might succeed and decay; nations might rise and fall without the masonic edifice, being affected; it has gone through past ages and will go through ages yet to come, always shedding on them lights and benefits.

It is however true that all our Lodges have not always worked with the same purity of principles; we have unfortunately seen the most culpable passions slip into them; intrigue has sometimes carried off that which merit alone ought to have obtained; personal interest has been allowed to succeed, when nothing but universal charity should have been listened to; the funds of the lodges have been diverted from their destination and they have not always been very scrupulous as to the means of augmenting them; but it is the abuse of the thing and not the thing itself.

Will they say that liberty must be renounced because they have caused it to degenerate into licenciousness? must we cease to preach equality because the principle might be made use of to break in pieces the salutary yoke of the laws. Ought one to despise logic because there have been sophists? and ought the morality of divers religious systems to be held less precious because their ministers have misinterpreted the meaning of it to satisfy their private interest? No, my brethren, the abuse of a cause ought not to occasion its rejection. If corrupt men are unfortunately introduced into our order, far from yeilding to them our Lodges by a cowardly abandoning, let us run there with zeal, armed with whips let us drive away from its sacred bosom those speculators and profaners who pollute its sanctity by making it a place of trafic and debauchery. Bring back by your fervency and your perseverance those happy times when all masons formed, really and from the heart but one family of brethren, united by ties of ardent and active charity, that the symbols that here strike our sight may not be a vain parade, a spectacle, wich I will dare to say would become ridiculous if they spoke not to our souls.—Let us distinguish ourselves rather by our virtues than by our decorations: that our actions may prove the purity of our morals, in a word let us be true and faithful masons, it is the best means of reducing our detractors to silence, of obtaining the approbation of the wise, and of meriting to be one day admitted into that heavenly and everlasting lodge wherein presides the G∴ A∴ of the U∴.

—The Spontaneous and reiterated bursts of applause which succeeded the oration, testified to the W. B. who had delivered it, the high satisfaction which had been inspired by a discourse so well calculated to strengthen their affection for the Order, and excite in their minds a firm resolution to remain steadfast in the practice of its principles.

8
LIST OF MEMBERS
Of the Grand Lodge of the State of Louisiana.

JOHN HENRY HOLLAND, Deputy Sheriff of the Paris Orleans, R. A., R. & S. M., K. T. Past Grand Master, G Master.

AMEDEE LONGER, merchant, R. A., K. T. ex-senior G Warden, Deputy Grand Master.

M. FOUCHE COUGOT, merchant, R. A. senior Grand War

J. BAPTISTE FAGET, freeholder, R. A., K. T. Junior G Warden.

JEAN F. CANONGE, lawyer, Secretary of the house of Re sentatives of the State of Louisiana, R. A., K. T., ex-G Master.

F. DISSARD, Preceptor, R. A., S. M., K. T., Grand Secreta

LOUIS H. FERAUD, lawyer, notary, R. A., S. M., Grand T surer.

ANATOLE PEYCHAUD, lawyer, Adjutant and Inspector geral of the militia of the State of Louisiana, R. A. K. T., Orator.

ADOLPHE W. PICHOT, lawyer, R. A., S. M. senior G Deacon.

SAMUEL D. DIXON, Druggist, R. A., S. M., K. T., Ju Grand Deacon.

F. JEAN VERRIER, merchant, R. A., Grand Steward.

FREDERIC BUISSON, farrier, R. A.   Ditto.

SAMUEL S. RELF, merchant, R. A., S. M., K. T., Sword rer, or Master of Ceremonies.

JOSE ANTONIO ROCA Y SANTI PETRI, a Military Emi R. A., K. T., Grand Marshal.

SETH W. NYE, collector and Port Warden, R. A., R. S. M Inside Tyler.

THOMAS LARTIGUE, M., Outside Tyler.

MEMBERS OF THE GRAND LODGE,

Holding no Office in the Same.

LOUIS C. MOREAU LISLET, lawyer, Founder, past Grand Master, R. A., K, T.
YVES LE MONNIER, doctor of medecine, Founder, past Grand Master, R. A., K. T.
AUGUSTIN MACARTY, freeholder, Founder, past Grand Master, R. A., K. T.
ALONZO MORPHY, attorney-general, R. A., S. M., Ex-Deputy Grand Master.
CHARLES MAURIAN, lawyer, Presiding Judge of the City Court, R. A., K. T., ex-Senior Grand Warden.
JEAN BAPTISTE LABATUT, merchant, Founder, R. A.
ETIENNE BERTEL, freeholder, Founder, R. A., K. T.
GEORGE WASHINGTON MORGAN, sheriff of the parish of Orleans, R. A.
JOSEPH CALISTE CONGOURDAN, contractor, R. A., K. T.
JEAN BAPTISTE PLAUCHE, merchant, R. A.
J. MANUEL FLEITAS, freeholder, R. A., K. T.
F. X. MARTINEZ Y PIZARRO, R. A., K. T.
CHARLES L. GARNIER, merchant, R. A., S. M., K. T.
JACQUES VIENNE, merchant, R. A., K. T.
LOUIS ALEXANDRE FAUSTIN DE BODIN, officer of the bank, R. A., S. M.
GABRIEL HENRY DE LÉAUMONT, officer of the bank, R. A.
NICOLAS LESCONFLAIR, contractor, R. A., K. T.
LOUIS J. DUFILHO, Jr, apothecary, R. A., K. T.
PIERRE ANTOINE ROUSSEAU, Custom-house officer, R. A., K. T.
HENRY H. DENIS, lawyer, R. A.
PIERRE CHEVALIER, apothecary, R. A.
JEAN BAPTISTE GILLY, merchant, R. A.
BARTHELEMI BACAS, contractor, P. M.
PIERRE BLANCHARD, dentist, P. M.
ALEXANDRE PHILIPS, merchant, R. A., S. M., K. T.
PIERRE DUBAYLE, teacher of languages, R. A., S. M., K. T.
JOSEPH BARABINO, apothecary, R. A., S. M., K. T.
ANTOINE BARBE, merchant, R. A., S. M.

10

J. B. BALTAZAR PLAUCHÉ, freeholder, R. A., S. M.
JOAQUIN VIOSCA, merchant, R. A.
GUILLAUME A. MONTMAIN, freeholder, R. A., S. M., J
W. R. FALCONER, Druggist, R. A., S. M.

HONORARY MEMBER,
M. P. G. MOTTIER LAFAYETTE.

OFFICERS REPRESENTING THE LODGES
Under the Jurisdiction of the Grand Lodge.

No. 1.
- H. R. DENIS, — W. Master
- FELIX FORMENTO, Doctor, R. A., — Senior W:
- M. FOUCHE COUGOT, — Junior W:

No. 3.
- A. PEYCHAUD, — W. Master
- B. B. KELP, — Senior W:
- B. D. DIXON, — Junior W:

No. 4.
- L. H. PERAUD, — W. Master
- F. BUISSON, — Senior W:
- H. JOHNSON, merchant, R. A., R. & S. M. — Junior W:

No. 5.
- J. H. HOLLAND, — W. Master
- F. J. VERRIER, — Senior W:
- J. B. PAGET, — Junior W:

No. 9.—Its Charter is Forfeited.
No. 10.—P. DESSARD, Proxy.
No. 12.—J. F. CANONGE, Proxy.
No. 13.—Not represented.
No. 15.—J. F. CANONGE, Proxy.
No. 20.—Has returned its Charter.
No. 23.—L. A. F. DE BODIN, Proxy.
No. 24.—R. F. Mc. GUIRE, Proxy.
No. 25.—Not represented.

No. 26.
- JOSEPH LONGBOTTOM, merchant, M. M.
- JOHN TYFFE, marble carver, R. A.
- ERASTUS BALL, merchant, R. A.

No. 27.
- J. A. ROCA Y SANTI PETRI,
- LINO DE LA ROSA, merchant, M.
- RAFAEL PEREZ, merchant, M.

No. 28.—J. H. HOLLAND, Proxy.
No. 29.—BLAIR Proxy.
No. 30.—J. H. HOLLAND, Proxy.
No. 31.—Not represented.

No. 32.
- ALEXANDER M'KEEVER, Inspector, R. A.
- JOSEPH S. M'FARLANE, Doctor, M.
- JOEL ASHLEY, merchant, R. A., R. & S. M.

No. 33.—Not represented.
No. 34.—Not represented.

11
LIST OF THE LODGES

Under the Jurisdiction of the Grand Lodge.

La Parfaite Union, No. 1, sitting in the city of New-Orleans.
La Concorde, No. 3, - - - - - - - - - ditto.
La Persévérance, No. 4, - - - - - - - ditto.
L'Etoile Polaire, No. 5, - - - - - - - ditto.
L'Etoile Flambotante, No. 10, Baton-Rouge. (Louisiana.)
La Verite, No. 12, Donaldsonville, - - - - - ditto.
L'Union, No. 13, Natchitoches, - - - - - - ditto.
Columbian, No. 15, Alexandrie, - - - - - ditto.
L'Humble Chaumiere, No. 19, St. Landry, - ditto.
L'Union, No. 23, Parish St. James, - - - - - ditto.
Western Star, No. 24, Monroe, (Ouachita), - ditto.
Lafayette, No. 25, New-Orleans, - - - - - ditto.
Harmony, No. 26, ditto, - - - - - - - ditto.
Numantina, No. 27, ditto, - - - - - - - ditto.
St. Alban, No. 28, Jackson Parish East Feliciana, ditto.
Harmony, No. 29, Opeloussasville, - - - - ditto.
Lafayette, No. 30, Vermillonville, (Attakapas.) - ditto.
Feliciana, No. 31, St. Francisville, - - - - ditto.
Louisiana, No. 32, New-Orleans, - - - - - ditto.
Hiram, No. 33, Cheneyville, - - - - - - ditto.
Selected Friends, No. 34, Clinton, - - - ditto.

Days of the Sittings of the Lodges in New-Orleans.

La Parfaite-Union No. 1, first Sunday in each month.
La Concorde No. 2, fourth Sunday in each month.
La Persévérance No. 4, fourth Sunday in each month.
L'Etoile Polaire No. 5, first and third Sundays in each month.
La Triple-Bienfaisance, No. 20, first Sunday in each month.
Lafayette No. 25, second Sunday in each month.
L'Harmony, No. 26, first and third Sundays in each month.
La Numantina, No. 27, first and fourth Thursdays in each month.
La Louisiana No. 32, first and third Tuesdays in each month.

12
RESOLUTIONS AND AMENDMENTS.

RESOLVED, That hereafter no Charter shall be granted the constituting of a new Lodge, until the application shall l laid over one meeting, and the day for the final consideration be fixed at the first meeting at which the petition shall have l read.

RESOLVED, that no Brother who has been elected to any ce in the Grand Lodge, shall have the right to decline the cepting said nomination, unless she hall have filled the same p during the preceding year.

RESOLVED, that when at elections of the first four office the Grand Lodge, no Brother shall obtain a majority of all the tes, on the first ballot, the second ballot shall be between the highest, and if it should to happen that the result of said b should produce the same number of votes for more than two Brot then the subsequent ballots shall be between the two who ar nior members of the Grand Lodge.

EXPULSIONS DURING THE YEAR 1829

By the lodges under the jurisdiction of the Grand Lodge of State of Louisiana.

By Lodge No. 4, Gatien Mortimer, for anti-masonic cor and immorality.

By Lodge No. 5, J. F. C. Bouchet Riviere, for anti-ma conduct.

By Lodge No. 25, Edouard Lafitte, for anti-masonic cor and non payment of dues.

By Lodge No. 27, Juan Iñacio Caballero, ditto, Jean G, eraced from the list of the Gd. Lodge for getting away undo charge of a fraudulous bankruptcy,

By Lodge No. 29, Th. S. Saul, for anti-masonic conduct.

By Lodge No. 30, P. H. Parrot, ditto.

By Lodge No. 31, Robert Colfax ditto.

EXPULSIONS COMMUNICATED BY SEVERAL GRAND LODGES

By the Grand Logde of Pensylvania.

By No. 72, John Alexander; 169, Samuel C. Allen John Amberg; 59 A. W. Banes; 60 William Beazell; 72 W Boheim, Blackall W. Ball; 82 Henry Baznes; Joseph B; 123 Daniel Bailey; 155 Thomas Brock; 156 Banker; 178 Ri Bard; 166 Samuel Budd; 196 George Brandner; 21 G. F. 82 Enos Cook; 116 John Camp; 151 George Cowl; 164 l

13

Callow; 46 Sames Dunwoody; William Dain; 179 Ferdinand Dutell; 194 E. R. Dartnell; 82 Isaac Everett; 116 A. L. Evans; 128 Job Eldridge; 186 Thomas B. Emory; 60 Robert Fee; 82 W. J. Freele; 9 Patrick Garvey; 21 William Greer; 123 Jacob Gochenour; 132 William Griffith; 60 James Hustings; 82 Jobias Hornbeck; 138 John Roseby Hann; 155 Daniel Hesser; 156 Jacob Heiss; Robert Hayes; 169 Christian Heastant; 182 Hugh R. Hunter; 186 William Hore; 60 Robert Johnson; Edward Jordan; 155 Jeremiah Jones, Thomas Inskeep; 67 William Kimbert; 946 Hineas Kelly; 143 Jonathan Keyser; 177 James King; 82 Christopher Longstreth; 116 H. C. Longland; Michael Lentz; 155 Joseph Laforest; 189 Harsy Lyman; 21 Benjamin D. Moyer; Isaac M'Cord; 128 George M'Leod; 156 Jacob Moore; 179 James M'Malk; 185 Elijah D. Mack; 187 Charles Mann; 197 William Main; 64 Paul Neigh; 123 T. O'Hail, 83 S. Persons, J. L. Parsons; 102 T. N. Penrose, 142 J. Philipps; 155 B. Patton, S. Pryor; 156 W. Parher, 82 J. Quick, 82 J. Reynolds; 128 David Rickifus; 46 Absalon Sellers, 66 R. E. Shannon, 123 J. Smyth, 132 J. W. Sparks, 156 Augustus Scoten, 169 Michael Screin, 194 Jesse Snyder, 83 A. Tyler, J. Tyler; 91 J. B. Taylor, 116 James Jhompson, 155 Robert Thomas, S. H. Tinker; 171 T. Thomas, 155 V. Vanholt, 158 C. Vansyck, 81 J. Zane, 82 M. Wolf.

By the Grand Lodge of Vermont.
By No. 55 David Adams, 6 Otis Frary, 19 Isaac French.

By the Grand Lodge of Kentucky.
By No. 25 David M. Alexander, 55 H. D. Atchison, 51 W. Buckner, 56 Willis Bates, 72 T. F. Bradford, 74 S. Bowling, 56 Robert Cartey, 69 Reubin J. Eastin, 18 J. J. Griffith, J. Holt; 78 Elijah Harris, Zechariah B. Malone; 65 S. Norton, 1 J. Stivers.

By the Grand Lodge of Virginia.
By No. 48 Benjamin S. Adams, 121 Robert Anderson, 129 T. L. Amis, 135 Henry P. Arnal, 18 W. G. Andrews, 87 J. Allen, 3 J. H. Brewer, 52 Richard P. Bolling Dr., 55 Daniel Brown, 96 Alexander Boyol, 68 J. Crummey, 87 W. D. Christian, 117 J. Crandall, 127 J. H. Cocke, 13 W. Dulaney, 21 J. Dewar, 105 Edwards Leroy, 129 Berton Elkins 87 F. Hill, T. Hill, 96 Edward W. Henry, 110 Sames H. Hereford, 129 Douglass W. Hardin, 105 Charles Lamkin, 21 Elias March, 131 W. Marshall, 18 Charles Newell, 119 J. Nanse, 6 S. Presson, 21 W. Powell, 3 Natha-

Lux e tenebris

www.ingramcontent.com/pod-product-compliance
Lightning Source LLC
Chambersburg PA
CBHW031142160426
43193CB00008B/227